WEARDALE

IN OLD PHOTOGRAPHS

WEARDALE
IN OLD PHOTOGRAPHS

—— COLLECTED BY ——
JUNE CROSBY

ALAN SUTTON
1989

Alan Sutton Publishing
Gloucester

First published 1989

British Library Cataloguing in Publication Data

Weardale in old photographs
1. Durham (County). Weardale. Social life,
history
I. Crosby, J.H. (June Hilda)
942.8'64

ISBN 0-86299-694-5

Front cover illustration.

THESE QUAINT IVY-COVERED HOUSES were once part of the buildings grouped around the mill at
Frosterley. The sash windows are later insertions. A tiny original window survives near the
corner of the house in the foreground and indications of a much steeper pitch to its roof on
the adjoining chimney suggest it was thatched before having its stone flag roof. All has gone
now; even the little stream lies buried beneath Mill Lane. (Mrs L. Aberdeen.)

Typesetting and origination by
Alan Sutton Publishing.
Printed in Great Britain by
Dotesios Printers Limited.

CONTENTS

LANE HILL AND WHITESTONES, near Ireshopeburn. A typical Weardale scene; long views across to the tree-bare moor; miles of dry stone walling outlining the patchwork of fields below; a tree-lined burn; a cluster of stone-built homesteads sheltered by trees; and traces of former industrial activity. (Mrs J.H. Crosby.)

INTRODUCTION

Until recently, Weardale was the unknown North Pennine dale hidden, as an early writer quaintly claimed, like 'a pearl in an oyster – or honesty in a poor house'. Certainly, 'Weardale' does not conjure up the instant image evoked by The Yorkshire Dales or The Lakes. Yet, in variety and beauty of scenery, it can challenge that of those better known areas and, by those who know it, it is at least equally appreciated.

Streams from the wild sparsely inhabited moorland of the Pennine water-shed come together above Wearhead and the River Wear starts to cut its way down the Dale. As it flows, it is joined by a succession of burns, such as those of Swinhope, Wellhope, Middlehope, Stanhope, the Fine Burn and Waskerley. Below Wolsingham, the valley widens out and the Wear eventually flows past the grandeur of Durham to the once great shipbuilding yards at its mouth.

But the lower Wear Valley is not Weardale. Weardale is the upper valley extending down as far as the eastern outskirts of Wolsingham. It is an area of considerable mineral wealth – lead, ironstone, a little silver and limestone.

Weardale is an historical as well as a natural entity. It is encompassed by the ancient parishes of Wolsingham and Stanhope. The area comprised the western estates of the Bishops of Durham before the Norman Conquest and so, ecclesiastically, economically and administratively, the Dale was a defined region, with Wolsingham as its first 'capital'.

At first, Weardale was used primarily as a hunting park by the early medieval bishops. West of Stanhope, over 30,000 acres in Stanhope Park and Forest Quarter were reserved for deer. The annual autumnal 'Great Hunt' – so often depicted only as a major social event – provided venison for salting and drying for use during the winter months and culled the animals, so giving the remnant a better chance of survival to the next spring. The Boldon Book, an 1183 survey of the bishop's estates, lists the many duties imposed upon the bishop's tenants to ensure that the hunt was properly organized. Some had to provide hunting dogs, some rope, some transport, some the timber and labour for erecting a hall, privy, kitchen, larder and dog kennel. Three wood-turners of Wolsingham had to provide 3,100 trenchers.

As early as the thirteenth century the hunting-park character of the Dale was being changed. Clearing for summer pasture in the upper Dale (often indicated by 'Shield' or 'Shieling') heralded the beginning of stock farming, a process largely completed by the late sixteenth century.

Exploitation of the Dale's mineral wealth also began early. Bishop du Puiset was given the mineral rights by his uncle, King Stephen, in c. 1160. There is evidence for lead mining from 1190, five centuries before large-scale mining by companies such as the London Lead Company and the Blackett–Beaumont group. A 1567 inventory of John Featherstone (of Stanhope) shows that he had been buying lead and stocking it at Hartlepool, presumably for export.

So, very early on the dual character of the Dale was established – a mixture of the industrial and the agricultural – which persisted into the twentieth century. The small farmer/miner was common in the Dale. 'At Stanhope they are chiefly farmers and miners whom they call groves' wrote Bishop Pococke in 1760. Quarrying too was established early; stone was required for larger buildings such as Stanhope Old Hall and the churches, if not for smaller houses; limestone was burnt for fertilizer.

The Black Death, in making labour scarce, loosened the firm hold the bishops had over the tenants, especially where obligatory duties were concerned. The political and religious changes of the sixteenth century also loosened the bonds and Bishop Matthew's attempt in 1595 to tighten his control over tenure was of limited success. By this time, Weardale people had acquired a reputation for independence and had been described as more stout than wise, more stubborn than well counselled. There was trouble in the mid-seventeenth century also, when the Bishopric was abolished by the Puritans and the new major landlord, Sir Arthur Heslerige, also found it difficult to enforce his will on tenants. At the Restoration, Monarchy and Bishopric were re-established and Weardale shared in the so-called Great Re-building of late-seventeenth-century England, as farms such as Wester-hope and Wiserley Hall indicate.

Parliamentary enclosure during the eighteenth century produced the many miles of dry stone walling going up to the fells, and the large-scale exploitation of lead began. This late-eighteenth-century Weardale was the one seen by John Wesley when he came and initiated an imprint upon the Dale still discernible today. In his journal he wrote, 'The green gently rising meadows and fields on both sides of the little river, clear as crystal, were sprinkled over with innumerable little houses; three in four of which, (if not nine in ten) are sprung up since the Methodists came hither'.

London Lead Company came into the Dale and made a tremendous impact upon the built and the natural environment. Stanhope was the Weardale centre and Stanhope House and adjoining buildings, cottages in the Butts and a workshop area were introduced by the company. The lead tithes were so considerable that the Rectory of Stanhope came to be the 'golden living'. Up the Dale, the Blackett–Beaumont company headquarters were at Newhouse, Ireshopeburn, and St John's Chapel emerged as an important upper Dale centre as a result. These two companies made the Dale fully industrial. As they declined, quarrying came to the fore during the nineteenth century and resulted in the further expansion of villages such as Frosterley and Stanhope.

Photography appeared in the Dale around 1855 and caught the Dale at a comparatively late stage of its history. But the camera recorded not only the then contemporary scene, but often indicated the inherited past. It came at a time when the Dale was predominantly industrial and just when the introduction of the railway was to lead the Dale out of its isolation.

A mid-nineteenth-century writer said of the people of Weardale, 'There is a strong good feeling and deep sincerity to be found among them. The occupation of mining naturally leads to reflection ... they are marked by a firm spirit of independence; and many of them evince considerable intellectual activity and acquirements'.

The sturdy stone buildings of the Dale are a reflection both of the natural environment and the people themselves. Undoubtedly, the isolation of the Dale, the dangers of mining, the hazards of quarrying and the unpredictable fortunes of farming have helped to create an independent, caring and versatile community and one with a wonderful sense of place. Life for many was hard until after the last war, yet resilience and creativity emerged, backed by the Methodist ethos.

Music flourished in nineteenth- and early twentieth-century Weardale – bands, musical societies and choirs. There was a strong tradition of versifying – one part of Newlandside Quarry was known as 'Poet's Corner'. Libraries were well used and there were many societies connected with poultry, pigeons, gardening and fishing, and games were highly popular.

As quarrying and mining declined, out-of-Dale opportunities beckoned – in Tees-side whose new industries offered employment, and further afield in America and the 'colonies' (South Africa, Australasia, Canada). Many Weardale people took advantage of assisted passages and cheap or free land to seek a fresh start. Yet most retained links with the Dale – often in the summer we have visitors seeking people, places and memorials of their Weardale roots.

And again, though many young people leave the Dale, by choice or necessity, many keep contact and return in later life. Old family names in the Dale, such as Emerson, Peart, Nattras, Cruddas and Walton, among others, survive today. So Weardale retains even now a strongly individual identity and a strong sense of continuity.

Many homes in the Dale have collections of local memorabilia, photographs, letters from emigrants, pamphlets and books by local authors such as William Morley Egglestone, J.J. Graham and John Lee. Bowes Museum has a collection of fine photographs taken by a former vicar of St John's Chapel; Beamish Museum an outstanding collection of photographs, mostly of mining and quarrying in the Dale. The Weardale Museum of High House has a growing collection of Weardale photographs. So the collection of photographs in this book is but the tip of the iceberg; but it is hoped that it will portray the many facets of Weardale from 1860 onwards and illustrate a little of its history.

First Impressions

THE NATURAL ENVIRONMENT

SWINHOPE FALLS, near Westgate, C. 1940. The many falls along the Wear and its tributaries in the Dale are a delight to walkers and naturalists. Vegetation is surprisingly lush – sycamore, ash, alder, willow, hazel, birch, rowan and (occasionally) bird cherry flourish, as do marsh marigolds, wood anemones, primroses, bluebells, cuckoo pint and the trenchant broad-leaved garlic. As a result of pollution, fish stocks were sadly depleted; for the past 20 years however, the Northumbrian Water Authority has been restocking the river with sea-trout and salmon with encouraging results. At Swinhope Falls a fish pass has been made (near the right bank in this photograph) to allow fish to pass upstream during the breeding season. (Miss N. Dawson.)

BRIGGEN WINCH, Stanhope, c. 1930. Usually called Stone Bridge, this high-arched bridge has been called the Fairy Bridge and the Roman Bridge. The latter description at least is inaccurate. Built before 1500 and widened in 1792, the bridge has always been a vital link in communications, for Stanhope stands at a crossroads which links the up-Dale road with Teesdale to the south and Edmundbyers and Blanchland to the north. (Mrs E. Forster.)

THE FALLS IN STANHOPE DENE, c. 1910. 'Dene' is commonly used in the north-east. Originally meaning a vale, it has long been used only of the deep, narrow and wooded valley of a small stream. The Dene at Stanhope is just that. In this photograph Miss Mary Mason sits reading in the sunlight of an Edwardian Sunday afternoon. In 1914 she married George Backhouse and lived in School House (really Boxwood Hall), where she had been born, for her father had also been headmaster of Stanhope Barrington School. (Miss B. Backhouse.)

WIDLEY FALLS, Stanhope Dene. Photograph on glass, c. 1880. Widley Falls can be anything from a fierce cascade to a mere trickle. They fall around 60 ft; the ferns, so beloved of the Victorians, still flourish in the cracks and crevices nearby. (Mrs L. Aberdeen.)

THE RIVER WEAR near Wolsingham, 1942. By contrast with the preceding three photographs, many stretches of the Wear are wide and placid. Such places are favourite picnic and paddling spots but the revetting on the nearside bank indicates that even here the river can show another, uglier, mood. (Durham County Reference Library.)

NOW ONLY USED BY THE OCCASIONAL ANGLER OR PADDLER, the former ford at the foot of The Butts was well placed for access to the Market Place, c. 1920. Apparently there was a rough causeway here as recorded in 1777 when footpads, having robbed Captain Ward of Newlandside and Thomas Robinson of Bushey Flatt, fled across the causeway tearing up planks behind them to hinder their pursuers. The high sloping wall with its semi-circular buttress behind the boys was erected by Dr W.H. Robinson to protect his home from flooding. Robinson claimed that, in 1890, he stood safely behind his wall and washed his hands in the flood waters swirling past. (Mrs J.H. Crosby.)

MORE PROPERLY BRITTON (NOT BRITTAIN) BRIDGE, this is a footbridge at the western end of Westgate beyond the present caravan park. Originally built in c. 1935 it replaced the old stepping stones of Shallow Ford which, with the ford for horse traffic, had served for at least a century previously to link the village with Hill Houses and Windyside House. Britton Hall, a substantial building on the lane leading from the main road to Shallow Ford, is now subdivided into four houses. (Miss N. Dawson.)

ERECTED IN 1768 THE OLD STONE BRIDGE, Wearhead, was badly damaged in the 'Great Floods' of 1771 which were so severe that only one of the many bridges crossing the Wear from source to mouth was undamaged; many were destroyed. Widened in 1810 to cope with increased cart traffic, the bridge was in bad repair and an accident 'black spot' by 1900. It was replaced by an iron bridge just before the First World War. This card was one of the 'William Morley Egglestone' series printed by S. Tinkler of Stanhope. (Mrs E.E. Carrick.)

CORONATION BRIDGE across the Wear, Stanhope, c. 1939. This graceful suspension footbridge, built in 1902 to commemorate the coronation of Edward VII, was swept away in fierce gales in April 1947 and replaced by the present bailey bridge which was erected by the army. It offers an alternative to the stepping stones across to Unthank Hall and the river walk to Crookledy Path. Each September the bridge is extremely busy when local families and visitors cross to the Agricultural Show, 150 years old in 1990. (Miss B. Backhouse.)

KENNETH'S BRIDGE was erected 1936–7 from timbers used in building Burnhope Reservoir. 'Kenneth' was K.R. Maddison, cabinet-maker and joiner of Frosterley, who built it. Lime production was increasing at the Broadwood works and the Bishopley kilns were being refurbished, having stood idle since 1919. These offered much needed employment and the bridge was a convenient route for men crossing to work. Kenneth's original bridge was badly damaged by flood in 1947 and had to be strengthened. It was rebuilt c. 1968, but traces remain in the bank. (Mrs M. Walton.)

THE IRON BRIDGE, Wolsingham; erected in 1894 by Durham County Council. Of the first medieval bridge nothing is known except it was replaced c. 1470 by a stone bridge of five arches. This was swept away in the Great Floods of 1771 and replaced by another stone bridge with two arches, which lasted until the present Iron Bridge replaced it. (Mrs J.H. Crosby.)

THE DALE CAN ONLY BEGIN when 'Harperley roundabout is at your back'. Above Wolsingham the Dale stretches before you, an ever changing vista to which nowadays the Eastgate chimney, when caught in the evening sun, can add a dramatic accent. Although so important environmentally, the river is no help to communication. The up-Dale road and branches off (such as Wearsbank, Wolsingham, above, c. 1920) are the Dale's life-lines, threading together its settlements and giving access to the outside. (Mrs J.H. Crosby.)

THE ROAD UP THE DALE – through Frosterley, c. 1930. Front Street was officially the Lobley Hill Road as it was maintained by the Gateshead turnpike trust of that name in the early nineteenth century; nevertheless old photographs suggest that the road from Wolsingham to Stanhope and beyond was still a dirt road until after 1900. (Miss N. Dawson.)

THE ROAD UP THE DALE – through Stanhope, c. 1895. 'Lime Tree Walk' is an impressive approach to the Market Place and pleasantly softens the high stone walling. The trees are indicated on a plan of 1826 but just when they were planted is not known nor by whom – various rectors of Stanhope are usually given the credit. The inner of the two lines of trees (nearer the Market Place) has gone, though a remnant of one juts out of the gable end wall of Mr Harry Perkins' shop. (Mrs E. Hall.)

ROADS IN THE DALE The up-Dale road winds through Ireshopeburn (above) and on to Wearhead and Cowshill. At Ireshopeburn it is joined by the back road (in foreground) from St John's via Hauxwell Head, and the hill road (far distance) snaking its way past Newhouse, originally called Short Thorns; this name was transferred to the farm cluster (middle left), once an inn. (Miss N. Dawson.)

THE ROAD UP THE DALE — Cowshill, 1953. This is the Dale in summer mood, pleasant and inviting. The hill beyond the village climbs towards Sedling, a lead site since 1457. The detached house on the right is still 'Miller Thompson's house'. Thompson's generosity during the 'hungry forties' of the last century enabled many local families to survive the terrible hardships of unemployment and high prices. (Mrs A. Dargue.)

THE OPENING OF THE NEW ROAD from Eastgate to Rookhope, 1913 — the horse still reigns. The road up the Dale follows very roughly the same general route as it did in the thirteenth century. Branches off the main road are also old, many of them determined by fordable crossings over the river. (Stanhope allegedly stands at a prehistoric crossroads.) Compared with these this new road is new indeed, being a mere 76 years old. (Mr A. Blackburn.)

SLIT WOOD AND MIDDLEHOPE BURN, Westgate: one of the Dale's special places. Leafy Slit Wood takes its name from the Slit Vein which was rich in lead and iron, and Middlehope was once an important mining area. From 1801–78 four mines were worked here by the Blackett-Beaumont Company: Middlehope Shield, Slit Pasture, Middle Slit and Low Slit. From c. 1810–26 the London Lead Company was also mining in Middlehope. Low Slit's main shaft was one of the deepest in the Pennines. At the time of closure, the Beaumonts were driving a new deep level 4 miles along Slit Vein from near Camuckeels. Middlehope is peaceful now, but the water wheel pit, the engine bed and bouse bays are visible reminders of its industrial past. (Miss N. Dawson.)

ON THE MOORS ABOVE WHITE KIRKLEY. Exploring the White Kirkley area is one of the numerous walks to be enjoyed in the Dale and, like most of them, offers a variety of scenery. Climbing up the narrow road from the tiny hamlet (population 36 when this photograph was taken) one passes Low Bishopley, an outwardly modest farmstead but once a minor bishopric hunting lodge. Hiding within it are some remarkable cruck beams. Here, wide open views are the walker's reward. Then into the shelter of this plantation with an occasional glimpse of a red squirrel and the call of cuckoo and woodcock. Then down to the narrow and secretive Fine Burn and, beyond that, an expanse of heather moors. A typical Weardale walk, part of which has been beautifully caught by J.H. Lambert's photograph of 1942. (Durham County Reference Library.)

THE SILLS, Waskerley (sometimes Wascrow) Beck, Wolsingham, c. 1940. 'Sill' is a geological term for a bed of rock, used locally of small cascades of water tumbling over such outcrops of harder rock. Beck and Waskerley ('the valley of the stream') are words of Norse origin. (Durham County Reference Library.)

THERE ARE MANY TALES OF HARSH DALES' WINTERS, of sheep flocks decimated (as in 1947 in Swinhope when 12 sheep and a lamb were the pitiful remnant of a flock numbering over 150 before the snows), of houses cut off (as in 1937 when houses near Westgate were isolated for ten days) and of shepherds lost for hours in blizzards (as in 1931 when Walter Craig of Jolly Body Farm, Stanhope, carried his exhausted brother Leslie for miles ending up at Blanchland station). Yet there is no doubt that the Dale takes on a new magic when covered with snow. (Miss M. Carrick.)

THE MARKET PLACE AND TOWN HALL, Wolsingham. The present market place area developed towards the end of the late seventeenth century. From 1763 there was an annual 'Hiring' and cattle fair. Revd W. Wilson (Rector 1789–1843) initiated a market improvement scheme including a Town Hall, completed in 1831 with an open-sided lower storey for stalls and a meeting room above. Although the building line around the Market Place is roughly the same, the buildings have seen many changes. George Race's imposing Primitive Methodist Chapel, erected in 1885 to seat 400, replaced the thatched house and forge of Minikin the Blacksmith. Opposite the east end of the Town Hall (altered beyond recognition) the former Royal Oak and thatched Cross Keys were transformed into the Mechanics Institute with its library of 1,400 books. The modernized Institute is now the Workman's Club; the Chapel has been sold off, its stone lettering obliterated, and nearby houses have been drastically altered. (Mrs J.H. Crosby.)

EAST END, Wolsingham, c. 1900, probably the oldest part of the town, for the market was held around here from the first market charter of 1508 until 1667. Meadhope Street and Silver Street still retain an atmosphere of rural village charm unaffected by later industrial development. Yet within the houses tucked away from the bustle of the Market Place there remains, thankfully, no trace of the other side of the old rural 'charm' – the shared pump or communal outside tap, the ash-pit netty, the 'poss' stick and the jug (of cold water) and ewer for washing on frosty mornings. (Mrs J.H. Crosby.)

FROSTERLEY – the 'forester's clearing' – was a Norman foundation; in 1183 it was held by Ralph Cant for half a mark. Observant visitors can spot 'two' Frosterleys; the old Frosterley centred around the shrunken village green and the once all-important mill; and the newer, nineteenth-century Frosterley with rows of miners' and quarrymen's houses. This photograph looks east towards the old Frosterley. On the left is the 1878 Methodist Chapel which was closed in 1978 and demolished and replaced by two houses in 1983. Left of centre is Wilf Robinson.

HILL END, NEAR FROSTERLEY, 1940. This cluster of snug cottages has magnificent views so it is not surprising to find that many are now holiday cottages or second homes. Nor is it surprising to find them there, clinging to the edge of the moorland, for the area abounds in traces of lead mining and smelting, and limestone quarrying which provided work, thus creating the need for houses here and at Whitfield Brow and Bollihope. (Both Mrs M. Walton.)

A VIEW ACROSS STANHOPE.

> Wolsingham's full of pride and 'that a donnet'
> Frosterley's hungered and has a good stomach
> Shitleyside stands in a row;
> Stanhope's the bonniest town o' them o'.

No doubt the originator of this rhyme (of unknown name and date but pre-1815) was a Stanhope man, but the town does offer a bonny prospect nestled in the shelter of the hills. (Mrs E. Hall.)

EAST END, STANHOPE, represents a largely nineteenth-century extension along Front Street. Dales Terrace on the left, which includes Kingston House, the former home of William Morley Egglestone, was built upon fields called 'The Dales'; dale here being an old northern version of dole or share, and refers to a very early division of land. (Mrs P. Craggs.)

24

THE PANT, Stanhope Market Place, before 1930. Pant is an old northern word for fountain. The one at Stanhope was given by Revd William Darnell, Rector 1831–65, to provide pure water for people living nearby, and was refurbished around 1885 by Dr Charles Arnison of Butts House; it was removed in 1934.

THIS BRIDGE CONNECTED STANHOPE CASTLE to the ornamental and kitchen gardens on the other side of the road. Designed entirely for convenience and privacy, Cuthbert Rippon was said to have used it around 1835–49 to escape from many pressing creditors. The bridge was demolished in 1963 to allow for road improvements and to permit the passage of large lorries up the Dale to the new Blue Circle Cement works at Eastgate. A Dales Centre is to open in 1990 in the gardens once served by the bridge. (Both Mrs L. Aberdeen.)

PLANS AT STANHOPE for a police station and Town Hall, complete with court-room, were prepared as early as 1846. The Rector, the Revd W. Darnell, was actively involved and the Bishop of Durham gave the land at West End. It was 1861 before police station and Town Hall were built; in the meantime the building, now the West End Co-operative store, served as a police station and lock-up. A new Town Hall was erected in 1901 alongside the old which became part of the police buildings; it is now a community centre. (Mrs L. Aberdeen.)

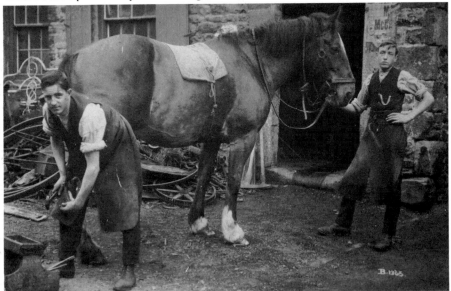

STANHOPE SMITHY, C. 1905. The blacksmith was a skilled and valued craftsman, and this one was nicely placed at Crawley foot and next door to the Grey Bull. The low building, with its monolithic door and windows tucked under the eaves, is a familiar Weardale type. (Mrs James.)

TOLL COTTAGE, Greenfoot, Stanhope. This picturesque cottage still survives though a little altered; it was a toll cottage collecting dues from travellers. Sometimes called Galleys locally after the family pictured here who lived in the cottage around 1914, it is now part of the Greenfoot caravan site. (Mrs P. Craggs.)

THIS EARLY PHOTOGRAPH shows Front Street, Westgate, before 1874 and before the Institute was built. (Mr K. Fairless.)

WESTGATE STATION was lovingly cared for by its railway staff; three times they won first prize for the best kept station and garden. Here Jack Snowdon and Harry Watt pose with understandable pride beside a flower bed which reads 'by rail, 1*d*. per mile, any train, anywhere'. Round their necks they wear the tablets ready to hand on to the driver of the next train. This was a safety device on single-track railway to ensure that the track was clear of any train coming in the opposite direction. Photograph before 1942. (Mr K. Fairless.)

ST JOHN'S CHAPEL MARKET PLACE – after the war memorial was erected in 1920 and before the bridge over the Harthope Burn was widened. In the background is St John's Church. Founded before 1465 it gave its name to the settlement, sometimes referred to as 'Weardale St John'. The square pyramidal capped tower belongs to the rebuilding of 1752. St John's became a separate parish in 1866. (Weardale Museum.)

EAST BLACK DENE AND CHESTERS. The hamlets of East and West Black Dene were thirteenth-century clearances for pastoral farming, the early beginnings of a three-century process which eroded the hunting park character of Upper Weardale. The stone walls are the result of Parliamentary Enclosure of 1799, while the hamlet still retains much evidence of mining activity. Prys and Chesters developed in the late-eighteenth century as overflow areas for the growing population of East Black Dene. (Miss N. Dawson.)

MAIN STREET, Ireshopeburn, 1957, showing John Dawson's home (now The Weavers) on the far left, beyond the former café and next door to the Institute. The up-Dale road swings sharply right in front of Midlothian House. The narrow road past the Institute climbs towards Lane Hill and the Causeway Road. Though removed from John and Shirley's wedding album, the photograph does not show Ireshopeburn as it was on that day. Heavy snow transformed the scene and much digging out preceded John's journey to church at Stanhope. (Mrs E. Hall.)

THE ROAD UP THE DALE, Daddry Shield, c. 1918. This illustration was taken from a slide belonging to Mr K. Fairless of East Haswicks. As some of the houses on the right have long since vanished and the original photograph is lost, this picture is something of a rarity.

Post Office, Wearhead.

'AT WIERHEAD begins the cultivation and the appearance of a few trees' wrote a traveller from Alston in 1804. This photograph, 120 years later, certainly suggests a pleasant rural retreat and many such quiet places still abound; but not near this former post office, now surrounded by later building around the eastern approach to Wearhead Bridge (just rebuilt in 1989). (Mrs E.E. Carrick.)

BLACK DENE AND BRIDGE, date unknown, with nineteenth-century miners' cottages. The two-arched bridge was built in 1848 to connect the village to Ireshopeburn. In July 1983 the bridge was badly damaged by floods following torrential rain and a garage, built on to a row of houses nearby, had the swollen Sedling Burn flowing over its roof. (Mrs L. Aberdeen.)

A CORONATION YEAR PHOTOGRAPH of the hamlet of Burtree, near Heathery Cleugh, one of a series taken to commemorate the Coronation of HM Queen Elizabeth II in 1953. Burtree, allegedly derived from the Weardale name for the Elder, gave its name to the Burtree Dyke, an impressive basalt outcrop. (Mrs A. Dargue.)

COWSHILL, 1,300 ft above sea level, now presents a rural scene fitting its name; in the nineteenth and early twentieth century it was a mining and quarrying centre. A nearby quarry has partially cut setts suggesting that the workmen have just finished for the day. The Cowshill Hotel occupies a prominent position and has been an inn for at least 140 years. (Mrs A. Dargue.)

ROOKHOPE showing the original 1823 church in its village setting; the church was demolished 1904–5 and much of its stone was used in the building of a new church, St John's, on higher ground. The old church was unusual: it was not aligned on the usual east–west axis and, although called Holy Trinity by some, it was never formally dedicated. (Mr A. Blackburn.)

THE FIRST CAR AT ROOKHOPE in front of the inn, c. 1920. The bearded man is John Cruddas, the landlord, whose father had been landlord before him and whose grandson is John Cruddas, the well-known landlord of the Grey Bull, Stanhope. (Mr K. Fairless.)

LONELY WELLHOPE has a thin line of scattered farmsteads running up its course. Their only link with the rest of the Dale is still the stony track leading down to the 'old Crag gate' about two miles away. Down this track Mr John Emerson, seen in this photograph with his sons Tom and Fred, took his stepdaughter (seated in the open trap) to her wedding with John Vickers Peart of Goldhill. (Mrs B. Emerson.)

FOR CENTURIES the horse was the mainstay of the Dale community, for travelling, for carting and for farming. Although unable to compete with steam and internal combustion engine it is, nevertheless, fitting that this section should open with the ever useful horse. (Mrs N. Brooksbank.)

THE OPENING OF THE WEAR VALLEY RAILWAY LINE in 1847 encouraged the introduction of the Mews horse bus to link the rest of the Dale to the railway terminus, first at Frosterley and, after 1861, at Stanhope. The coach (here at St John's Chapel) travelled 'up-bye' and 'down-bye' twice a day. The service ended when the railroad was extended to Wearhead in 1895. The coach 'Rob Roy', was stored at the Packhorse Inn, Stanhope, and used for special occasions until just after the First World War. It is now in York Railway Museum. (Mrs L. Aberdeen.)

THIS COACH AND PAIR is very superior compared with a farmer's pony and trap. Yet cart, trap, bus or a fine equipage all depended on the ever useful horse. This photograph was given to the Weardale Museum by Mrs G. Angus. The firm of 'Hodgson and Angus' is still a respected firm of solicitors in Stanhope, having been established there in the West End by George Walton Hodgson about a century ago. The Hodgsons lived in Westgate and it has been suggested that the man standing by the rear wheel of the coach is George Walton Hodgson, and that Westgate House is the building behind the coach.

THOUGH NOT USED AS MUCH AS HORSES, donkeys were used for light carts as this photograph demonstrates. It was taken c. 1920 at the foot of Wear's Bank, Wolsingham, near the iron bridge. (Durham County Reference Library.)

EARLY GPS IN THE DALE, such as Doctors Charles Arnison and William Robinson, travelled 20 miles or more a day. For visiting isolated farms a sturdy Dales pony was best. Robinson trained his pony, Tom, to help him open and shut farm gates without dismounting. For travelling on the main road a light pony and trap could be used, such as this one waiting (allegedly) for Dr J. Bourne outside Woodbine House, Ireshopeburn. (Weardale Museum.)

HORSES, AS CARS, could be used for pleasure as well as for work and here, in their Sunday best with trim pony and trap, the Vickers family enjoy a pleasant Sunday afternooon ride 'over the tops' to Haydon Bridge, c. 1920. (Mr A. Blackburn.)

THE INTRODUCTION OF THE STEAM RAILWAY to the Dale brought tremendous benefit transportwise although, at first, the line was not extended beyond Frosterley and the main emphasis was transportation of goods rather than passengers. This photograph of Wolsingham station shows the old stone bridge down Wear's Bank and over the river to the causeway, and the road bridge over the railway line. (Durham County Reference Library.)

WOLSINGHAM STATION-MASTER JOHN PETTY poses outside the station buildings with his family and staff in 1893. In the board room of this station (now a house) the company finally decided to extend the line to Stanhope in 1862 and to Wearhead in 1895. (Durham County Reference Library.)

It's all along the railway
'Hurrah' let dalesmen shout.
For now the line of rails is laid,
The railway's opened out.
From Wearhead to Stanhope town
Let waft on every breeze,
A hearty ringing cheer
To greet Sir Joseph Pease.
All along the railway
In sunshine and in shower
Up among the Weardale Hills
Sixty miles an hour.

(Weardale Museum.)

ENGINE NO. 69868 standing at Stanhope station. The last regular train from Wearhead ran on 27 June 1953. Stanhope station was closed in 1965. It was a sad end compared with the expectations of 1895.

Station Bridge & River, Westgate-in-Weardale.

WESTGATE STATION was built across the river from the village at Haswicks and reached via a bridge crossing the Wear and the railway line. On the hillside beyond the station are Park View, Rainey Close and Hill Houses. The station area is now much changed, having been turned into a club house, with tennis courts and football pitch. (Mrs J.H. Crosby.)

A QUARRY ENGINE on 'the Rolley Way', Parson Byers Quarry, 1921. Railroads were of great benefit to the quarries both on site and as links to the markets and processing plants. Among this group are Isaac Gowland and schoolboy W.R. Bainbridge. (Mrs I. Bainbridge.)

OUTSIDE THE STATION HOTEL, the Causeway, Wolsingham, c. 1920. Horses rest wearily with their loads of sandstone from the Redgate Quarry near the approach to the station. (Durham County Reference Library.)

A TRAIN DERAILMENT at Harperley, 1911. Fortunately of rare occurrence, such incidents attracted great local interest. (Durham County Reference Library.)

THE INVENTION OF THE INTERNAL COMBUSTION ENGINE also helped open up the Dale. It has been suggested that the occurrence of 'Weardale Goitre' gradually died out because close inter-marrying declined as public transport opened up possibilities for socializing further afield. This photograph and the one below show the development of the Rookhope bus service. The first Rookhope bus, c. 1925, was kept by George Vickers Baty who garaged it in the old corn mill. Mrs Hannah Baty, a yeast dealer, ran a carrier service to Stanhope on Saturdays.

THE 'LAST' ROOKHOPE BUS exhorts us to 'Drinka pinta milka day', a snappy slogan which outraged the pedantic during the mid-1960s; beside it stands an intermediate model. (Both Mr A. Blackburn.)

THE CARRIER TRADE was much improved by the motor vehicle and, whereas Joshua Dawson has his horse and cart at the turn of the century, Mr Hugh Featherstone Dawson in c. 1932 was able to offer the services of his cattle haulage truck, UP 7384, seen here behind Woodbine House. He also had a horse charabanc for excursions and a pony and trap 'taxi' often hired by Methodist Ministers preaching away from home. (Miss N. Dawson.)

THE INTRODUCTION OF THE CHARABANC (literally a 'carriage with seats') brought a relatively cheap means of travel to people unable to afford a car or a pony and trap of their own. This photograph of an early open-top charabanc, c. 1916, came from Mr K. Fairless' collection.

HORSE AND CAR CO-EXISTED for many years on the roads. Here a farmer and his cart approach the petrol pumps but he has no need of their Esso or Shell, c. 1935. This view of the main road through West End, Wolsingham, is clearly recognizable today, although the petrol pumps have been removed. (Durham County Reference Library.)

EVEN AFTER THE SECOND WORLD WAR, many Travellers were still using their horse-drawn caravans as they travelled the road; now, modern Travellers use a car and modern style caravan while old wooden caravans such as the one illustrated here, c. 1936, are museum pieces. (Durham County Reference Library.)

HORSE-DRAWN CARAVANS were sometimes used for holidays in the inter-war years. This family chose a caravan in the Dale for health reasons. They enjoyed the 'good air' and delighted in 'fetching milk fresh from the cow', but their table-cloth and other comforts indicate that they were not prepared to experience the true Traveller life-style. (Mrs L. Aberdeen.)

BICYCLING BECAME EXTREMELY POPULAR from the late 1870s as the cheapest form of private transport. The lad seen here appears to have a machine with a chain and pneumatic tyres – refinements introduced in the late 1880s. He was photographed on the Causeway, Wolsingham, c. 1914, near the Crofts, on which modern council housing has been built. Fosters Lane was an older name for the Causeway. (Durham County Reference Library.)

THE WOLSINGHAM CYCLING CLUB, shown here in admirable array, was but one of numerous clubs which proliferated during the 50 or so years before the mid-1930s. Cycling clubs offered companionship and opportunities for excursions away from the familiar scene. Gradually, modern roads, faster cars and greater prosperity eroded their popularity. (Durham County Reference Library.)

STEAM, CAR, BICYCLE — yet still the horse has his following and the Dales pony, so long the only form of transport in the Dale, is still lovingly bred — as this recent photograph, taken from the Stanhope Agricultural Society's archives, of Mr Tom Coulthard and his prize animal indicates.

ORIGINALLY BUILT BY GEORGE PEARSON OF DURHAM in 1790, Harperley Hall was owned by his heirs the Wilkinsons (1798–1892) and the Stobarts. Pearson and his son-in-law G.H. Wilkinson were noted award-winning 'improvers'. The pleasant scenery around Harperley is their legacy. Wilkinson also extended the Hall. It is now a police training centre. (Mrs J.H. Crosby.)

FAWNLEES, one of the many fine period houses around Wolsingham, indicates the town's former importance and prosperity. Its mellow 1787 façade masks a much longer history; it is listed in Bishopric estate records from c. 1359. (Durham County Reference Library.)

BISHOP OAK — another beautiful house near Wolsingham — also has an early eighteenth-century façade and a tall summerhouse which belie its true age. Held by the Curry family from Elizabeth I's reign until 1890, it then passed to a distant relative, Mr J.E. Milburne, who kept the Corner Garage, Wolsingham. He sold Bishop Oak to the Featherstone Fenwick family in 1925. (Durham County Reference Library.)

WHITFIELD HOUSE, guarded by its holm oaks, is the finest house in Wolsingham's main street. The adjoining stone-mullioned Whitfield Cottages (1677) are equally attractive. Kiln House, where John Wesley stayed in 1754, is on the corner. Joseph Wooler of Fawnlees had 'Whitfield House' cut high on its façade c. 1905. In around 1925 it was a boarding house kept by Mrs Mary Ann Watson. (Mr and Mrs W.H. Holden.)

THE WATSON FAMILY has farmed Baal Hill for over 60 years; before them the Wearmouths and Rogersons, all continuing a tradition of at least 450 years. In 1558 Bishop Tunstall's officers paid £18 16s. for repairs to the Lodge called Baylehillhouse in the Bishop's Park at Wolsingham. Within the present farm, so pleasantly situated and affording lovely views, hidden features such as barrel vaulting and thick walls indicate a still earlier history for this intriguing building. (Durham County Reference Library.)

IN CONTRAST with many other houses in the Dale, Leazes House at Wolsingham is not an ancient building with its origin in the Bishopric estates. It is a comparatively modern, late-nineteenth-century house built by Mr C. Bainbridge whose father founded the very first department store. The house became a sanatorium for TB patients in 1909 with Dr Menzies as MO, and Miss Muschamp and Miss Coates as Matron and Deputy. It is now part of Wolsingham Comprehensive School. (Durham County Reference Library.)

A NINETEENTH-CENTURY TERRACE stands on Dam Hill, once the dam bank of the Frosterley Mill mill-pond. On the right-hand end is the former blacksmith's shop. The people: on the left are Tommy and Frances Briscoe with young George Harrison; next door is Tom Dowson, holding Tiny the dog; then Ida and Nelly Harrison and the Gibson family – Bella, Margaret, Oliver, Mrs Gibson and Joseph. Photograph c. 1920 (Mrs L. Aberdeen.)

TODAY, IMPOSING STANHOPE OLD HALL is subdivided and used as a hotel and private home. It reveals evidence both inside and out of a 700-year progression of architectural styles. The complex still indicates its original character of a self-sufficient estate with old water corn mill, threshing floor, barns and brewhouse. The home of the Featherstonhaughs in ancient times, it passed to the Earls of Carlisle c. 1730 and to Cuthbert Rippon MP c. 1830. Later, the Ecclesiastical Commissioners purchased it but sold it off during the present century, since when it has been associated with the Dale families of Collingwood, Turnbull and Mews. Photograph c. 1930. (Mrs E. Forster.)

ENLARGED AND MUCH ALTERED INTERNALLY, Stanhope Castle was an approved school from 1941–1981. The photograph was taken by a member of staff c. 1947. The Castle is now divided into private apartments whose residents enjoy the lovely parkland setting. (Miss M. Carrick.)

Stanhope Castle 110 years Ago

'STANHOPE CASTLE 130 YEARS AGO', i.e. 1835, shows the gentleman's residence originally built by Cuthbert Rippon, a London solicitor, in 1798. It was enlarged by his son Cuthbert, the first MP for Gateshead, who was forced by his creditors to sell the house in 1857. Hardly anything is known of the appearance of the original castle; already ruinous by the early fourteenth-century, it may have been a basic Norman motte and bailey castle with a wooden keep. (Mr and Mrs J. Adamson.)

STANHOPE CASTLE LODGE is tucked away behind the arched drive entrance. In contrast with the classical style of the big house, the lodge is lightly Gothic. Photograph c. 1920. (Mr and Mrs W.H. Holden.)

STANHOPE HOUSE, c. 1920. This pleasant house was designed by Ignatius Bonomi and built in 1819 as the official residence of the local manager of the London Lead Company who sold it to the Walton family in 1855. It has been the Rectory for the incumbent of St Thomas' since 1957. (Mrs E. Wearmouth.)

THE OLD RECTORY, Stanhope, when the Revd J. Shebbeare, chaplain to HM the King, was Rector (1921–42). It was designed by Bonomi and built at a cost of £12,000 for the Revd H. Phillpotts, Rector 1821–30, when the Stanhope living was one of the richest in the country. The Rectory survives but is now divided into church hall, flats and a house. The fine view from the terrace is still there but, below, the heated greenhouses, the shrubberies and the flower and vegetable gardens have been replaced by a caravan park. (Mr J. Shebbeare.)

BUTTS CRESCENT, Stanhope. The curving line of The Butts was cleverly used in the design of this pretty terrace, built for ostlers working for the lead company. There is a touch of the Gothic style in the only original surviving door and fanlight. The door surrounds are surprisingly smart for modest provincial houses. (Mrs J.H. Crosby.)

NEWTOWN HOUSE, c. 1945. This area was known as Newtown long before Mr J.W. Roddam JP built his fine villa and formal gardens. In 1933 the then owner, Mr R. Kellet, converted it to a comfortable hotel with an open-air swimming pool. In 1951 the hotel was purchased by the County Council for women patients and is now a residential home. (Mrs J.H. Crosby.)

TUCKED AWAY ON THE 'BACK ROAD' near Eastgate is elegant Horsley Hall, once home of the Hildyards, a family prominent in the Dale for nearly 500 years. The house is now a hotel whose proprietor, Mrs K. Wagner, provided this c. 1920 photograph. The original seventeenth-century character of the hall has been retained, although it was considerably extended in the eighteenth and again in the mid-nineteenth century when Anthony Salvin (Croxdale-born architect) remodelled the front. In 1975 Mr Parnaby, the then owner, added a baronial hall to the rear with a roof removed from Cheeseburn Grange, Northumberland.

CRAWLEY HALL was built c. 1841 as a residence for the manager of the Consett Iron Company's Ashes Quarry. It is a substantial house overlooking the Dale from the treacherous Crawleyside Bank. Its occupants have included Walter Mallaby Townsend, Edgar W. Dakins and Dr J. Rhodes, former Head of History at Neville's Cross College, Durham. Emma Jane Askew was born here in 1885; her son, William Askew McAlonan, took this photograph with him when he emigrated to New Zealand as a souvenir of his mother's birthplace.

IN 1910 THE OLD 'BUG AND FLY' FARM (and sometime alehouse) was replaced by a 'neat villa' for the mines manager – a marked contrast to the rough and haphazard construction being revealed during demolition. A chance discovery by local miner Bell Patterson of an accessible vein of fine lead in 1895 had revived lead mining in Rookhope when many other mines were worked out. (Mr A. Blackburn.)

THE EVER USEFUL PONY AND TRAP is standing outside East House, Ireshopeburn. The house shows the 'polite' style of building in details such as pointing applied to the traditional stone building of the Dale, and the bay and sash windows; but, above the door, samples of 'spar' show a true Weardale touch. (Miss N. Dawson.)

THE EASTERLY END OF IRESHOPEBURN. On the extreme left is a mobile workman's hut parked prior to road works. The two neat stone houses on the right are Snapcastle and Brookside. Snapcastle is described as an old name by an early nineteenth-century writer. There are many such intriguing property names in the Dale – Seldomseen, Teetolly Hill, Miseryhall, Noah's Ark, Cold Knuckles and Jolly Body are a few examples. It is not surprising that Dale residents like to retain them. (Miss N. Dawson.)

A TERRACE OF BACK-TO-BACK HOUSES was built in Rookhope c. 1910. Each house had a small plot, its own 'netty' and an allotment nearby. It was given the name Hylton Terrace, but the villagers christened it 'Blue Row' because of the slates on the roofs — a material not used locally until after the railway had penetrated up the Dale and so provided a means to transport them. (Mr A. Blackburn.)

A ROOKHOPE SMELT WORKER AT HOME. Mr and Mrs Tom Gardiner of Simpson's Terrace sit beside the kitchen range — a fearsome thing to blacklead every morning, yet the family's source of warmth, hot water and cooking. The round oven was peculiar to County Durham and south Northumberland. The Gardiner's little girl in her laced boots sits beside them on a 'cracket', c. 1915. (Mr A. Blackburn.)

THIS CAREFULLY POSED PHOTOGRAPH of the interior of Lintzgarth, Rookhope, is beautifully evocative of the turn of the century. It is thought to be of a member of John Adamson's family who farmed Lintzgarth c. 1895–1930. There is a strong tradition of music-making in the Dale, particularly the upper Dale, which still persists today. The 'squeeze-box', organ, violin and piano were widely used. Here, the piano takes pride of place. (Mr A. Blackburn.)

MARY HANNAH DARGUE poses in a photograph of the farm kitchen at Rush where her parents John and Hannah raised four sons and six daughters. The Dargue's great-grandson, Jack, skilfully replaced the missing upper part of the dresser which, together with the violin and ornaments, are still special possessions in a home in the Dale. (Mrs A. Dargue.)

THE REVD JOHN J. PULLEINE, Rector of Stanhope 1888–1913, is shown at work in his study at the former Rectory, surrounded by all the paraphernalia of a well-to-do churchman – books, prayer desk, devotional pictures. (Miss B. Backhouse.)

SMALL UPLAND FARMS such as Old Dowks offer a stark contrast with the luxury of the Rectory and it is not surprising that, today, many are deserted and their holdings absorbed by other farms. Yet they arouse admiration for the people who lived and worked in them, for the ingenuity in devising 'built-in' shelving such as this and for the skill revealed here in building the dry stone walls. (Mrs J.H. Crosby.)

The Dale at Work

FARMING

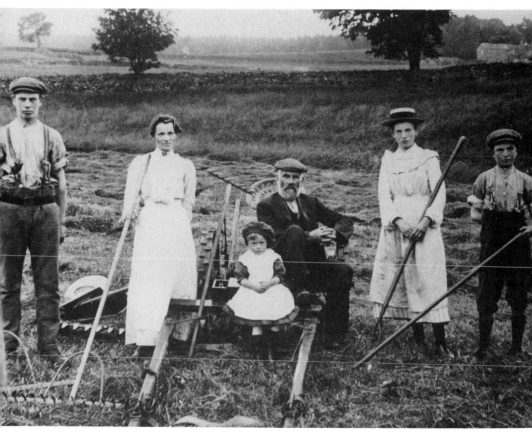

HAY IS STILL THE MAJOR CROP of the upland farmer in the Dale and vital for winter feeding. Traditional hay-making, where horse and man carried out the task, was a period of intense activity when everyone joined in to ensure that this essential job was done 'while the weather held'. Here the Dawson family make hay at Ireshopeburn, c. 1908. Left to right: Thomas Edwin Dawson, Sara Annie Dawson (née Peart), Leon Dawson (still unbreeked), Thomas Dawson, Mabel and Arnold Dawson. Little Leon when adult became a well-known singer in the Dale. (Miss N. Dawson.)

WESTFIELD FARM, Wolsingham, is typical of many Weardale farms — house, byres and stores in a long row, originally built into a bank for shelter and convenience with a few trees planted, again for shelter. Such low-lying farms are used for fattening sheep and cattle brought down from higher ground, and for sheltering ewes in lamb. Joseph Henderson was farming here at the turn of the century and Thomas Pickering around 1925.

HILLTOP, an upland farm at Lanehead, was formerly worked by the Dargue family. In the background is the five-arched bridge carrying the main road to Alston across the little steep ravine of Heathery Cleugh. The farmhouse has gone but the old byre remains and — sign of the times — has recently been purchased for conversion to a cottage. (Mrs A. Dargue.)

LONGLEY FARM (i.e., the long clearing) lies low south of the river and is seen here when still a working farm. Since 1963 it has been part of the Blue Circle Cement plant at Eastgate. Some of the farm buildings survive and are used by the works. (Mr and Mrs A. Pratt.)

WILLIAM JOHN CURRAH, in his summer Sunday best, admires a fine ewe and her lamb outside Parson Byers Farm, c. 1910. With him is his mother, Margaret Currah (b. 1844), the daughter of William and Anne Ridley of Peakfield, Frosterley. (Mrs M. Wilkinson.)

SHEEP SHEARING is a crucial time for the farmer and was very labour-intensive in the days of hand-shearing. Traditionally, it was also a social time when 'bait' (i.e., food) had to be taken out to the workers and when family, children and neighbours would turn up to watch, to gossip and to congratulate. (Mr and Mrs A. Pratt.)

OCTAVIUS MONKHOUSE, solicitor and keen sheep breeder, holds his prize Scotch black-faced ram at Chapel Show in 1924. Behind him is shepherd Robert Robson Milburn, widely known in the Dale for his breeding of an improved black-face. (Professor T.R. Milburn.)

A LITTLE GIRL, wearing her long plaid coat, proudly plays the careful shepherdess complete with proper crook. In the background, somewhat hazy, are the Wolsingham Steel Works, founded in 1864. Unfortunately, the date of the photograph and identity of the shepherdess are unknown. (Mr and Mrs W.H. Holden.)

THE ACQUISITION OF NEW STOCK, and so new blood, is always important to the farmer and here Joseph Currah of Parson Byers poses with his latest acquisition, c. 1930. (Mrs M. Wilkinson.)

CUTTING THE HAY using scythe and horse, between Westgate and Daddry Shield, c. 1910. The horse, rake and hand scythe were the haymaking 'harvesters' of the pre-tractor age, and many in the Dale can remember the old ways continuing long after more mechanized methods were available. (Weardale Museum.)

BEFORE THE DAYS OF POLY BAGS and automatic hay-bailers, the building of ricks had to be tackled after haymaking. This was a skilled job; ricks had to be protected from weather and made safe from fire. Here the Dawson family are building their ricks in Hotts Field, Ireshopeburn, c. 1914. (Miss N. Dawson.)

THE FAMILY AT GUARD HOUSE, Prysedale, pose in Sunday best in front of their completed ricks expertly built, roped and thatched to withstand winter storms. What a contrast to today's mechanized 'rolls'! The name Pryse is of uncertain origin but may hark back to the days when the Upper Dale was officially under forest law: 'to blow the pryse' was to give the signal on the hunting horn that a stag had been taken. (Mr A. Blackburn.)

PEAT CUTTING was confined to the upland moors. Three basic tools were required; a marking iron to cut into the top turf, a narrow spade with a projecting fin which enabled regular-size slabs to be cut and a long-handled, roughly triangular iron to lift the turf. After being dried the peat was 'stooked'. It is slow burning and smoky but was free to those with common rights. (Weardale Museum.)

DRIVING THE GEESE TO MARKET along the main road up the Dale at Wolsingham would not be attempted today. One could be excused for thinking that this photograph was taken before the motor car age, but the date is after 1920 as the war memorial near the Town Hall is in position. (Mr and Mrs W.H. Holden.)

THE CONTRIBUTION TO FARMING in wartime by women was given official recognition by the formation of the Women's Land Army – Mrs E. Davison began as a land girl at Bradley Hall and is seen here helping with the milking in 1950. Land girls in the Wolsingham area lived at a hostel in the Causeway. (Mrs E. Davison.)

PRISONERS OF WAR were also used to aid food production in both world wars. Here, German POW Gerald Alleures poses at Bradley Hall Farm in 1944 with a compatriot and an official from the Home Office sent out to check on POWs working on farms. (Mrs E. Davison.)

PEAKFIELD NEAR FROSTERLEY has been farmed since before 1183 when it is listed in the Boldon Book as part of the Bishop's estate as held by Belnuf of the Peak. The Ridleys have farmed here for nearly 200 years and, before them, the Todds who migrated to Teesdale. It is a charming house with several interesting features and it lies snugly on the rising hillside south of the river. 'North side, sunny side; South side, money side' is an old Dale saying. (Mrs M. Wilkinson.)

ROOKHOPE LEAD MINERS C. 1900 and their tools – the hammer to drive in the borer (held by the miner sitting down) and the pick. Clothes had to be tough – corduroy trousers, high-buttoned waistcoat, thick shirts with loose dropped shoulders and stout clogs.

THE BOLTSBURN SHAFT, ROOKHOPE, down which the miners, materials and small wagons (hence the rails) reached the working face. Regulations were introduced to improve the safety of early cages and there were different fitments to carry men and materials. (Both Mr A. Blackburn.)

HOPE BURN SHAFT was sunk on the hills above Rookhope for extra safety and for better ventilation and access to the Boltsburn Mine, as the rich lead flatts being exploited were a mile away from the main shaft. (Mr A. Blackburn.)

BOLTSBURN MINERS outside the East level of the mine around 1900–1905. The mouth of the level is on the extreme right. The sticks which some of the miners are holding were used to aid their balance when walking stooped underground or walking on the edge of the rail tracks in the mine. (Mr A. Blackburn.)

THIS GENERAL VIEW OF BOLTSBURN shows the dense industrial area in this little valley. While the working of the lead mines and the quarries produced employment, it also led to pressure on housing and to the risk of such diseases as silicosis. (Mrs L. Aberdeen.)

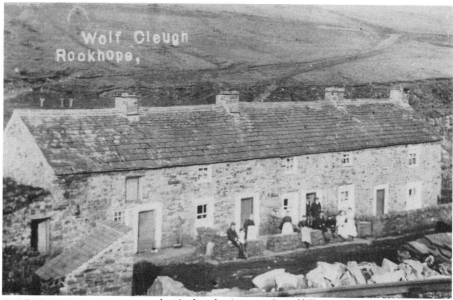

WHILE LODGING 'SHOPS' were used at isolated mines such as Killhope, the mine owners also built houses for miners and their families. This row was built at Wolf's Cleugh – where many traces of mining activity still survive. Water was fetched from spring or burn. A now lonely track over the moors climbs up behind the terrace. In the foreground, piles of stone await transportation along the lines. (Mr A. Blackburn.)

THE *LITTLE NUT* may look like a toy-train engine but it did good service on the Weardale Lead Company's 1ft 10in gauge railway linking Boltsburn Mine, the Dressing Mill and Lintzgarth lead smelter. Here, the *Little Nut* has its winter cab; its summer cab was open to the elements. The woman is standing against a snow plough which was fitted in snowy weather. She worked as a stoker on the *Little Nut* during the First World War when this photograph was taken.

GROVE RAKE MINE is one of the many mines in the Rookhope area and has been worked by three or four different companies. The Blackett-Beaumonts worked it 1819–83, followed by the Weardale Lead Company until 1916. British Steel Corporation worked it for fluorspar and closed it in 1983. (Both Mr A. Blackburn.)

TODAY, THE FASCINATING INDUSTRIAL ARCHAEOLOGY OF BRANDON WALLS lies hidden in the quiet woods of rowan, birch, hazel and bird cherry. Yet, in the nineteenth century, the lead mine and the lime kilns shown here, were busily at work; and this great 40 ft diameter wheel, then standing within its wooden cover, was used for driving water pumps in the shaft. (Mr A. Blackburn.)

IT IS DIFFICULT TO IMAGINE the leafy seclusion of Stanhope Dene as an industrial site, with 'an immense pall of smoke for ever hanging over it', but this photograph of the smelter, erected in 1845 by Charles Attwood, and the visible archaeological evidence still in the Dene indicate the exploitation of the Dene's lead, iron and limestone and, more recently, fluorspar. (Mrs P. Craggs.)

ROOKHOPE SMELTER WORKERS of 1902 in their work-a-day clothes; the head protectors were worn when the filthy but essential job of scraping out the long flues was undertaken, and some lead was retrieved at the same time. (Mr A. Blackburn.)

THIS PHOTOGRAPH OF WHITE'S LEVEL, Middlehope, c. 1900, shows the four great levers which pumped water used in the sorting of lead from waste. This was based on the simple principle that lead ore, being heavy, sank below the waste. White's Level was said to produce the best spar of all for the miners' ornamental carving. (Mrs J.H. Crosby.)

GANISTER MINER working at Rispey, c. 1930, with a wagon which carried the rock away. Ganister is 90 per cent silica, both hard and coarse-grained, and is used in brick making and hearth backs. (Mr A. Blackburn.)

BARBARY MINE, Ireshopeburn. During the 1960s fluorspar, once a waste product of lead mining, was seen as the future 'growth industry' of the Dale which would enhance employment prospects. These hopes have been only partially realized. The potential commercial value of fluorspar was recognized around 1885. John Coulthard is claimed as the first to exploit the Dale's fluorspar, his profitable business beginning with a 5 cwt spar from the waste-heap at Daddry Shield. Barbary, an old much-worked lead mine was reopened in 1905 and reworked for fluorspar and lead until closure in 1934. Weardale fluorspar is used in the making of Pyrex, of acid and as Freon in refrigeration. (Mr K. Fairless.)

WASHING LEAD ORE was one of the more unpleasant jobs associated with lead mining and was usually given to lads, some only ten-years-old.

> Cum ye little washer lads, Cum let's away,
> We're bound down to slavery for fower pence a day.

In the First World War, girls were employed as 'washer lads' and were provided with the thick overall, cap and stout clogs worn here. Like the men and boys, this girl carries her bait tin (lunch box) and 'tin' bottle. (Mr A. Blackburn.)

INDUSTRIAL ROOKHOPE in decay, c. 1950. The water wheel was still standing, disused and forlorn but, behind and to the right, a sign of hope – a crescent of council houses newly built after the Second World War. (Mr J. Brown.)

THE KNAPPING BENCHES in Ashes Quarry, around c. 1920. They are still easily discernible although the quarry has been closed since c. 1950. Some visitors assume that these benches carried a wagon way but the wagons ran below the benches from the quarry face and joined the track running up to join the Stanhope and Tyne Railway at Crawley Edge.

LIME KILNS, Crawleyside, c. 1920. Lime burning for fertiliser existed in the Dale for centuries but large lime kilns such as these belong to the industrial age. The development of the iron and steel industry led to increased demand for calcined lime, especially after the invention of the Bessemer process of making steel which was introduced to the Dale by Charles Attwood. (Both Mr J. Parmley.)

DEMAND FOR LIMESTONE AND LIME INCREASED during the First World War and workers were in short supply. Therefore the German prisoners of war from the camp at Shittlehope, Stanhope, were put to work at the quarries under guard. These are POWs employed at Ashes Quarry. (Mr J. Parmley.)

AN EARLY STEAM NAVVY and quarry-men with their foreman working at Parson Byers Quarry. (Mrs J. Wilkinson.)

STANHOPE QUARRY-FACE WORKERS pose with their manager, c. 1925. Stout footwear and thick clothing were essential; flat caps offered little protection against flying rock. Until the invention of the pneumatic drill and mechanical excavators, muscle power harnessed to hammer, pick, shovel and crowbar broke up the stone after blasting. Foremen carried an iron measuring ring to make random checks that the men were breaking stones to the correct size.

THIS EARLY RUSTON GRABBER, photographed at Parson Byers, helped to lessen the heavy labour of the quarrymen. It was, nevertheless, a hard life aggravated by unemployment and, to say a man was 'just a quarryman' was to grossly underestimate skilled and versatile men who took pride in their work. (Mr M. Wilkinson.)

THESE FOSSILIZED TREE STUMPS, discovered near the Edmundbyers road in 1914, are relics of the carboniferous age around 350 million years ago. Among the men who uncovered them were Henry and Elliott Stephenson, whose great grandchildren still live in Stanhope. One of the trees is on display in the Hancock Museum, Newcastle upon Tyne; another was moved to St Thomas' churchyard, Stanhope, by quarry owner Mr Beeston in 1962. Small pieces are to be found in many homes in the Dale. (Mrs L. Aberdeen, Mrs I. Bainbridge.)

QUARRYMEN HAD TO TAKE COVER when stone was blasted from the quarry face and then they returned to their 'benches' (left as working platforms) to cut and load the stone into the wagons. This photograph was taken at Parson Byers after blasting, c.1925.

'OFF DUTY' AT PARSON BYERS QUARRY, c. 1930. The quarryman's day began at 7 a.m., light and weather permitting, and ended around 5 p.m. There were two breaks from the heavy work — around 15 minutes at 10 a.m. for a drink of cold tea from a tin 'bottle', and a longer break for their 'bait' at lunch-time. (Both Mrs M. Wilkinson.)

GERMAN PRISONERS OF WAR working at Newlandside Quarry during the First World War. This quarry opened after the railway was extended to Stanhope in 1862 and a private side line was built to connect with the Wear Valley line. (Mr J. Parmley.)

THIS PHOTOGRAPH, c. 1917, belongs to Mr Jimmy Parmley of Stanhope who worked for many years in the quarries. Pick, shovel, hammer and crowbar were the basic tools of the quarryman at this time.

THE QUARRY FACE at Parson Byers c. 1950; this clearly shows the awesome height of the quarry and the different strata within the face. Strata in quarries were given local names by the workers such as Toby Giles, Mucky Post, Twee Toms and Dun Kit Post. Mr Ronald Priestman Wilkinson is talking to Mr Stanley Robson (in the shelter). (Mrs M. Wilkinson.)

THE EXTENSION OF THE WEAR VALLEY RAILWAY to Stanhope, and later to Wearhead in 1895, enabled Dale quarries such as Stanhope Heights and Haswicks to be worked economically. This photograph is of Stanhope Burn quarry, c. 1900. (Mr K. Fairless.)

CRAWLEYSIDE, a hamlet just north of Stanhope, began to expand in 1834 when the new Stanhope and Tyne Railway enabled limestone won at Ashes Quarry to be taken to ships at South Shields. Houses, school and church were eventually built; shops and pubs (the Sir George and the Crawley Inns) were opened. Shops, church and school have long since been closed. Of the pubs, only the upper one shown here, (now the Campbell Arms) still functions.

LEAD MINING has left so visible an imprint on Weardale that it is not surprising that it is often referred to as a 'lead dale'. Yet iron was also mined here and more iron than lead was worked between 1666 and 1938, the period of greatest commercial exploitation. Iron was mined in Stanhope, around Rookhope at Grove Rake and Fraser, and at Middlehope, where this photograph was probably taken. (Mr A. Blackburn.)

THE WOLSINGHAM STEEL WORKS at Stanners Close was a major employer in the town from 1864. Erected by Charles Attwood, the business continued under his nephew John and traded as John Rogerson & Co. until 1930. The works pioneered steel castings and made a major contribution to the war effort of both world wars. Electric arc furnaces were installed c. 1950, but trade gradually declined. Closure came in 1984 but a workers' co-operative continues the 125-year-old tradition in a small way.

CHARLES ATTWOOD (c. 1792–1875) of Hollywood Hall used the Bessemer process patented in 1856 to produce steel from Weardale iron at his new works. He boasted that, had he been a younger and fitter man, he would have made Wolsingham another Sheffield. He is buried in St Mary and St Stephen's churchyard, Wolsingham. (Both Durham County Reference Library.)

THIS OPEN HEARTH 25-TON FURNACE, for producing heavy steel castings and ingots, was one of four of this type of varying size used at the Wolsingham Steel Works during the 1940s. The largest castings were sent out by road. In May 1941 a large casting broke from its moorings and two workmen were pinned beneath it. Dr J. O'Hara had to carry out amputations before the men were freed. Mr W. Austin and Mr D. Crockett (Superintendent and Deputy of the Isolation Hospital) helped him; all three were given an award by the King.

A CONVERTER FOR STEEL REFINING in use during the 1940s at Wolsingham. This process was used for the production of a small type of steel casting as the molten steel could be made quickly and in relatively small quantities. It produced about $1\frac{1}{2}$ tons of molten steel at 40 minute intervals. (Both Durham County Reference Library.)

STERN CASTING for HM Cruiser at Wolsingham, believed to have been photographed in 1942. A variety of other goods including bomb cases, dredger tubs and train wheels were produced here (some claim that the 'Big Wheel' at Blackpool was also made here).

A MOULD FOR THE BOTTOM PART OF A CAST STEEL STERN FRAME at Wolsingham Steel Works, c. 1943. The top part was built up of boxes containing sand and one of these top portions can be seen in the background. It was for work such as this, and for stern casting and great anchors, that the Works gained an international reputation. (Both Durham County Reference Library.)

THIS FINE PORTRAIT OF AN UNKNOWN 'BASKET WOMAN' was taken by Miss Bessie Graham (c. 1910–1986). Shops, as we know them, are comparatively modern. First came the market stalls, the small local shops and the packmen or pedlars who (as here) plied their uncertain trade from fair to fair and farm to farm. In Weardale the travelling salesmen were known as badgers and they have all but vanished since the Second World War. Shops in the Dale are still mostly small family concerns though there is a Co-operative Society and, in Stanhope, a Walter Willsons. (Mr and Mrs W.H. Holden.)

THIS FRUIT AND VEG CART is outside Rookhope School which was erected in 1875. Such 'mobile shops' became commonplace in the later nineteenth century. The tradition is still continued in the motor-car age by retailers such as Woodhalls of Stanhope. Some Dale traders such as Mr Graham, the 'yeast man' of 70 years ago, used a horse sledge in snowy weather. (Mr A. Blackburn.)

TWO NATTRASS BROTHERS of St John's Chapel also had a fruit and veg cart for most horse and cart trade was in perishables. Nattrass is a name known in the Dale since 1427. In 1791, John Nattrass was one of the 12 local men who won permission from the bishop to open a Methodist Chapel at Westgate. Near that chapel (now three houses), a present-day Nattrass runs his butcher's shop and abattoir. (Mr and Mrs W.H. Holden.)

EVEN IN 'URBAN' WOLSINGHAM, horse and cart trade could make a living, for it was very convenient for a housewife so much more tied to house and housework than now. Presumably this trader sold more than just apples. Another Wolsingham man, Gibson Beadle, also plied a horse and cart during the inter-war years, selling fish and chips.

WOLSINGHAM IS A TRUE MARKET TOWN as it has had the right to hold a market since 1508, though the market was never very prosperous and had to be re-established in 1614 and again in 1667 when it was moved to the present Market Place. In the years before the First World War attempts were made to revive the market yet again; this photograph shows one of them. There is much bustle and excitement and the Union Jack is flying from a window of the former Queen's Head, but the enterprise had no long-term success. (Both Durham County Reference Library.)

THE MARKET CROSS was prominent in the Market Place, St John's Chapel, until it was demolished in 1865 when there were plans for a Town Hall. This opened in 1868. The weekly market continued but declined after 1900. By 1925 it was listed as discontinued. Photograph no later than 1865. (Weardale Museum.)

STANHOPE MARKET PLACE AND CROSS, C. 1930. Stanhope received its first charter for a weekly Friday market in 1418. It was re-established in 1669 when a market cross was erected in the Market Place. The cross was restored in 1871; its original shaft is preserved in the churchyard. There was a wooden shed used by stallholders which was demolished, probably during the 1880s. The market was still being held in 1895 but, by 1925, it had been discontinued. (Mr and Mrs J. Adamson.)

CO-OPERATIVE STORES with their fair prices plus a dividend proved very popular in the Dale. Wolsingham was served by the Tow Law and District Industrial and Providential Society. This store replaced Dobbinson's who moved their family joinery business to the former Briggs File Factory c. 1898. The Co-op closed in 1969 and the premises were converted into two houses. (Mr and Mrs W.H. Holden.)

THE STANHOPE AND WEARDALE INDUSTRIAL AND PROVIDENTIAL SOCIETY, founded in 1865, ran the other Weardale Co-op stores. Stanhope was the headquarters with branches at Frosterley, St John's Chapel, Westgate and Rookhope. This impressive new 'Store', with upstairs lecture room, was erected at Stanhope in 1908 when the 'divi' was 2s. 11d. in the pound. The Stanhope shop was sold in 1987 (when 'divi' was barely $2\frac{1}{2}$p in the pound) and two less splendid premises have been acquired closer to the Market Place.

THE OPENING OF THE NEW STORE at Rookhope was a proud day for the Stanhope Society and very beneficial for this somewhat isolated district. Photograph from before 1925. (Mr A. Blackburn.)

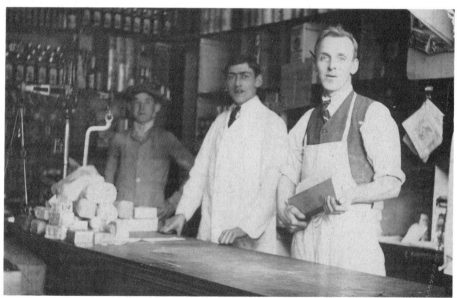

THE INTERIOR OF THE ROOKHOPE STORE on its opening day is captured here as the assistants pose for their souvenir photograph. (Mr J. Brown.)

FAMILY BUSINESSES such as Gallons of the Market Place, Wolsingham, vied for trade with the Co-ops. Prices displayed seem ridiculously low, c. 1905, but not when one remembers that a 'decent' weekly wage for a labourer was 17s. 6d. Lowes Tea and Dining Rooms next door offers 'cycle accommodation'. Facing up the street is the Beehive Grocery Store, now the Beehive Restaurant. All the buildings are recognizable today.

ROBERT WILLIAM PICKERING, 'Italian Warehouseman', stands with his staff outside his well-stocked shop in the Market Place, Wolsingham. His shop has a typical Weardale stone slab roof; all too rapidly many of these are disappearing. (Both Durham County Reference Library.)

MOFFAT'S SHOP, Front Street, Frosterley, served as drapers, grocers and post office, c. 1895, when it was run by Thomas Moffat and his wife. It became a mountain bicycle hire shop in 1989 after having been a hairdressers a few years earlier. (Mrs Ward, Cragside.)

SNOWBALL'S CHEMIST SHOP once jutted out into Stanhope Market Place but was demolished during improvements to the Market Place. Fenwicks were another occupant of this shop; they claimed to have been chemists since 1760. (Mr and Mrs J. Adamson.)

THIS PHOTOGRAPH of Thomas Phillipson's drapery and grocery shop in Front Street, Stanhope, is a lovely period piece. 'Phillipson Brothers, Grocers and Drapers' are listed in an 1895 directory. Thomas' name also appears in a 1925 directory, as trader and local magistrate. (Mrs L. Aberdeen.)

ANOTHER DELIGHTFUL STANHOPE SHOP FRONT. This little general dealers and sweetie shop was in Bridge Street, part of the main street beyond the Market Place which then ran under the bridge which linked two parts of the Castle grounds. Joseph Brownless ran the shop during the 1920s and before him, Mrs Brownless. The shop stood where the fire station and bungalows were built in c. 1968. (Mrs L. Aberdeen.)

STANHOPE POST OFFICE. The enamel sign and thermometer advertising Stephenson's ink were common during the inter-war years. When Mr and Mrs Leslie Adamson retired in 1987 they ended over a century of service to the Post Office by three closely linked families. Mr Adamson's father, George, had been postmaster 1947–62. He had followed Mrs Adamson's father, George Henderson, her grandfather, Joseph Henderson, and her great-grandfather, Maddison (1883–c. 1894), who were previous postmasters at Stanhope. (Mr and Mrs J.L. Adamson.)

FROM THE MID-NINETEENTH CENTURY until after the First World War, St John's Chapel was a
bustling little town with its Market Place shops, pubs and market serving the Upper Dale.
Here, Joshua Dawson IV had his drapery, grocery and general dealer's shop, which became
the only shop in England to be both post office and bank. Next door was the King's Arms
where Joshua III had been publican and first constable to the Association for the
Prosecution of Felons in 1820. Here also William Morley Eggleston had his printing shop
where he sold (among other things) barometers and concertinas, feeding bottles and
gunpowder, spectacles and pickles, fire shovels and violins, china and fishing tackle *and*
Blake's Antibilious Pill, 1*s*. 1½*d*. per box. There were other shops and pubs aplenty to provide
for local needs. (Weardale Museum.)

Bottom, left.

VILLAGE SHOPS had to be versatile in order to survive and provide for their customers.
Robinson's was such a shop; as grocer, draper, general dealer, post office and telegraph
office the Robinsons satisfied most ordinary needs of the Rookhope inhabitants. First
Thomas Robinson and then John Cameron Robinson ran the shop c. 1890–1926. (Mr A.
Blackburn.)

THE ISOLATION OF SMALL SETTLEMENTS before the rail and motor-car age meant that each community needed its own craftsmen such as miller, cobbler and smith. The mill in Slit Wood is now a secluded picturesque spot but once it was a busy corn mill and the path alongside it was the way to work for many miners. (Miss N. Dawson.)

THE DEMESNE MILL, Upper Town, Wolsingham, c. 1942. The Demesne Mill area is now a County Council picnic site and a pleasant spot for visitors to sit or stroll. As its name indicates, it was originally part of the land retained by the lord of the manor for his own use, here the lord was the bishop. All that remains of the actual corn mill mentioned in bishopric surveys of 1183 and 1381 are parts of its lower walls and, nearby, the remains of the mill race which brought the water to turn the water wheel. A corn mill was once absolutely essential to a community for it ground the rye, barley and wheat for making the bread that was the staple diet of ordinary folk until at least the 1870s. The former Rectory, near the church, was renamed Demesne Hall in 1988 when it became a residential home. (Durham County Reference Library.)

Bottom, left.
HUMBLE'S FORGE was one of nine small businesses in nineteenth-century Wolsingham powered by water, an interesting example of the first industrial revolution in action. In 1921 a water turbine was installed. The firm made spades and shovels for farm, colliery and industrial use. 'Ready-made' steel was obtained from ship-breakers' yards. First a tilt hammer and, from 1907, a steam hammer was used to forge the tools. The factory closed c. 1932; a caravan site and 1980s housing occupies its former site. (Durham County Reference Library.)

BLACKSMITHS were so essential for making and repairing the iron parts of farming implements and shoeing horses that settlements the size of Stanhope could still provide a living for two at the turn of the century: Robert Sisson of Crawley Foot here in the doorway with Norman his son, and Robert Dixon at West End. (Mrs Cilla Hobson.)

ROOF THATCHING in Weardale was heather thatching; heather was plentiful on the moors around and was free to the stint holders. An extra steep pitch to the roof of an old house often indicates that it was once thatched. None remains now, though a few thatched roofs survived into the twentieth-century. This photograph of a thatched cottage in Wolsingham Market Place was taken c. 1900. (Durham County Reference Library.)

BRIGGS FILE FACTORY in the Causeway, Wolsingham, specialized in high quality files, a basic tool widely used by smiths and mechanics. The overshot water-wheel seen at the right supplied the power; the arch supporting part of the workshop permitted the water to flow away. It is believed that the bearded man, wearing a hat in the foreground, is Joseph Briggs. 'Joseph Briggs file manufacturer Foster Lane' is listed as still working in 1895. The factory had closed by 1900 and the premises were being used by a joinery business.

THE CARTWRIGHT'S SHOP, Wolsingham. In the age of horse and cart, the cartwright or wheelwright was another essential craftsman as he built and repaired the carts, traps and wagons widely used for transporting goods and people. (Both Durham County Reference Library.)

MASONS CUTTING STONE TO BUILD A BRIDGE on the new road to Rookhope and, below, the bridge they built in 1913. Stone is the natural building material in the Dale and the centuries-old skill is displayed in churches and homes throughout the area. Unlike many other old crafts, that of the mason was kept alive by craftsmen of the previous generation such as Mr R. Hylton of Wolsingham who built the Grammar School there and Newtown House, Stanhope. The craft is kept alive today by craftsmen such as Mr George Martin of Hill End. (Mr A. Blackburn.)

THE DITCHER AND HEDGER'S TOOLS were simple – a billhook and a slasher. His skill lay in his hands, usually protected by a thick pair of mitts or 'dannocks'. Dry stone walling predominates in the upper Dale but lower down there was more work for hedgers and this photograph was taken in the Frosterley area, c. 1900. (Mrs J.H. Crosby.)

AS OLD CRAFTS DECLINED around the end of the nineteenth century, new jobs emerged. The Council became a prominent employer for maintenance work, refuse collection, sanitation and road works. This 1912 picture shows workmen laying a hard road surface near Wolsingham Market Place. The men are spreading small limestone which was then compressed by a steam-roller, sprayed with tar (from the horse-driven tar cart behind the steam-roller) and rolled again. This was 'laying the macadam' so called after the Scottish road builder. As always, road works attracted bystanders; here, mostly boys in their starched collars and knickerbockers; even the policeman is there with his bicycle too. There were three convenient public houses offering refreshment to the men after their heavy and dusty work – the King's Head (left), the Blue Bell (right) and the Wheatsheaf; none of which function now. (Durham County Reference Library.)

THE IDEA OF PARKS, BOWLING GREENS AND TENNIS COURTS for the general public gave new opportunities for leisure and also created new jobs. Bishop Pulleine provided the bowling green at Stanhope and the men here are rolling it for use. (Mr and Mrs S. Harrison.)

THE SECOND WORLD WAR brought new responsibilities and home defence was one of the more important. Here an ARP group stand 'at the ready'; some of them were part-time firemen, including Redvers Brown, third left. (Both Mr and Mrs Harrison.)

STANHOPE has had a part-time fire brigade since 1891; a water cart was their only appliance. Once a bell was rung in the Market Place to summon them to a fire; now they carry 'bleepers' and practice weekly in the custom-built fire station of the 1960s. Here, in the less sophisticated inter-war days, Redvers Brown, George Harrison and George Turnbull stand beside a trailer pump. During the First World War the fire appliances were stored in No.1 High Street; two rooms had to be knocked into one and the supporting arch inserted is now a feature of the occupants' sitting room. (Both Mr and Mrs S. Harrison.)

THE CAREER OF HAROLD STOREY (1869–1944) is an example of the emerging career opportunities in public service. A blacksmith's son, he became a policeman around 1895 and, from 1909 until his retirement, he was stationed in the Dale. He became a sergeant and, from 1923, lived in the house at Stanhope which is now the Community Centre. He retired in 1935, a highly respected Chief Inspector, and lived in Wolsingham at Hawthorn House (named after his birthplace near Seaham). His hobby was breeding cocker spaniels for which he won many prizes. He was also an active member of the Stanhope Silver Band and played the horn in their prizewinning London performance in 1934. (Both Mr and Mrs S. Harrison.)

THE BELL SISTERS HAYMAKING, St John's Chapel, c. 1914. These two photographs are from a fine collection taken by the Revd James Pattison, vicar of St John's 1905–1926, which may be seen at the Bowes Museum.

THE MAID at the Revd Pattison's vicarage taking in eggs at the kitchen door from a local farmer. On the wall hang the brushes for lime-washing – a way of keeping kitchens and outbuildings fresh and reasonably free of 'creepy crawlies'.

BEFORE THE FIRST WORLD WAR, opportunities for women in the Dale were confined to domestic service, farm work and marriage. This group of young women illustrate how times were changing: Ella Parker, lower left, trained to be a teacher at Darlington; Dulcie, Minnie and Muriel Place joined the Women's Auxiliary Army Corps. Dulcie later became a matron and Muriel a high ranking civil servant.

MISS NELLIE DARGUE proudly wears her academic gown and a badge of St Hild's College, Durham. She enjoyed a fine teaching career. She married John Stonehouse who rose in his work to hold a highly responsible position in the United Omnibus Company. (Both Mrs E. Wearmouth.)

SECTION THREE

People in the Dale

WEARDALE FACES

LOOKING AT OLD PHOTOGRAPHS OF PEOPLE has a fascination for many of us. They offer a tenuous link with the past and tempt us to guess at the personality behind the images of those who lived such different lives. Weardale has certainly reared hardy self-reliant people (such as the Dawsons) with a strong sense of family. It has also produced such characters as Joseph Sedgewick of Meadhope Street, Wolsingham, seen here when around 85 years old, c. 1895. Known locally as 'Jossy Siggy', he was a carter and, living at a time before the OAP had been introduced, he worked until he was well into his seventies. It is said he celebrated his birthdays by jumping over the mill race, only giving up the custom after his eightieth birthday, when he fell into the water. (Durham County Reference Library.)

MARGARET TAIT, a well-known Wolsingham character in the pre-1914 years, wears a sun bonnet type of hat much favoured in the Dale at the time. Her 'coat' is a plaid pinned round her shoulders (could it have been made at John and Robert Horsley's manufactory at West End?). Margaret raised four children on her own by charring. Yet local memory describes her as lively, loving a joke and 'a bit crack' (i.e., chat). (Durham County Reference Library.)

JOSHUA DAWSON IV (1821–1892). After a misspent youth this 'irrepressible sinner turned irrepressible saint' married Francis Tinniswood, became a substantial businessman and renowned evangelist Methodist preacher. He championed women preachers and a room over his shop in St John's Chapel was available for any woman forbidden to preach in the chapel. Unshakeable in his opinions, his portrait suggests kindliness as well as authority. (Weardale Museum.)

HANNAH DAWSON (1848–1923), c. 1873. 'I wish . . . you could have heard the complimentary remarks of some of the fellows here' wrote Hannah's fiancé about this photograph. Pale and quiet, she was also determined and steadfast, which is indicated by her fine strong face. Although the match was not welcomed by her father Joshua, she travelled to China in 1875 to marry Joseph Race and share the hardships of missionary life. Widowed, she returned to England in 1881 and often lectured on missionary topics.

RUSSELL TINNISWOOD, Florence Alberta and Joseph Dawson Race were Hannah and Joseph's children. 'Florrie', said her father writing from China, 'is a very bright little creature. I fancy she will develop a rather strong will . . . but as Hannah says "How could the child help having a strong will with such a grandfather and such a father?" '. Russell became a solicitor; Joseph, born after his father's death, became a banker. (Both Weardale Museum.)

THE WARDS OF CRAGSIDE, c. 1910. The Wards have held Cragside for nearly a century. Joseph Ward was farming the land in the early 1890s and was followed by his son. Joseph and his wife Elizabeth are pictured here with their son, John William, and their daughters, Margaret Elizabeth (Maggie) and Annie who migrated to Perdue, Sask. Cragside is a pleasant seventeenth-century farmhouse in the old Park Quarter of the Dale at Eastgate. It was held by the Bainbridges from c. 1800. Emerson Muschamp Bainbridge (1817–1892), founder of Bainbridges, was born here. In 1891 he endowed the Cuthbert Bainbridge Memorial Chapel in Eastgate in memory of his father. In 1975 the Bainbridge link was renewed when George V.M. Bainbridge opened a bazaar at the Chapel commemorating his great-great-grandfather. (Mrs Ward.)

JOHN DARGUE married Hannah in June 1852. Together they worked an upland holding in windswept Rush. In the tiny Hill Top farmhouse six daughters and four sons were born to them between 1854 and 1875. It must have been a hard struggle, yet neither of these photographs suggests people overwhelmed by their responsibilities. John's shows a pleasant man with a twinkle in his eye. Hannah's finely drawn face has great serenity while the details of her dress (crochet shawl, brooch at neck and neat cap) suggest a dainty woman. (Mrs A. Dargue.)

JOSEPH ASKEW, c. 1885. More is known about Joseph's brother John, the Stanhope cobbler and violin maker. However, a few relics of Joseph are cherished by his great-grandson and family in New Zealand, including this photograph and a letter he wrote from his home in Meadhope Street, Wolsingham, in 1885 to William John McAlonan, an 'incomer' to the Dale who married his daughter.

I give you our consent to marry our Daughter Emma Jane Askew. We hope she will make you a True and Faithful Wife and in return that you will make her a True and Faithful Husband ... with God's blessing hoping that neither of you will ever have to regret your Choice.

A WEARDALE FARMER: William John Ridley Currah in the garden of Parson Byers, the father of Mrs M. Wilkinson of Hollinside. Ridley was his mother's maiden name. Family surnames are widely used as forenames in the Dale. There are many examples such as Emerson Peart, Morley Egglestone and Priestman Wilkinson. (Mrs M. Wilkinson.)

NELLIE DARGUE, in Sunday best, was placed in a carefully contrived studio pose for this professional protrait, c. 1903. She was the daughter of Emerson Peart Dargue and Nancy Lamb, and the granddaughter of Joseph and Hannah Dargue of Hill Top, Wellhope. (Mrs A. Dargue.)

MRS WALTON OF STANHOPE HOUSE (now the Rectory) also poses somewhat stiffly, c. 1920. The widow of Robert Walton, coal and lead mine owner, she was an important lady in Stanhope. The stained-glass window in the Methodist Chapel was her gift. She is buried in St Thomas' Churchyard. (Mrs E. Wearmouth.)

MRS PRIESTMAN, Mrs Wilkinson, Mrs Carrick and Mrs Foster at Stanhope Castle School Sports Day, c. 1949. Stanhope residents were generally very supportive of the school. (Miss M. Carrick.)

A WESTGATE-IN-WEARDALE GROUP, c. 1895. Who were they? Why was the photograph taken? Alas, we do not know. (Miss N. Dawson.)

THE PLACE FAMILY outside Stone House, Stanhope, in the 1920s. Shorter skirts, shorter hair, this happy group shows how styles changed after the First World War. (Mrs E. Wearmouth.)

TOM M. SEXTON OF STANHOPE, Labour MP for Barnard Castle from 1935 (when he overturned the 'safe' Conservative seat held by Lt.-Col. Headlam) until 1945. His son Willard also attended Wolsingham Grammar School and a brilliant career was forecast for him; a successful barrister-at-law, he was chosen as Parliamentary candidate for Hexham. However, Willard died tragically young from a chronic illness apparently the result of blood poisoning from a pen nib while at school. Willard Grove in Stanhope is named after him and he is buried at Stanhope. (Mrs E. Forster.)

EDUCATION IN WEARDALE has a proud history. Wolsingham Grammar School was founded in 1614, Westgate School in 1681. Frosterley had a small free school founded by the John Hinks Bequest of 1735. There were several 'Hartwell' and 'Barrington' schools in the Dale. These were not sufficient, however, to provide the obligatory 'education for all' of the 1870 Act. This Board School at Bridge End, Frosterley, c. 1930, was erected in 1876 to provide some of the extra school places needed. It held 230 children and is still in use. (Mrs J.H. Crosby.)

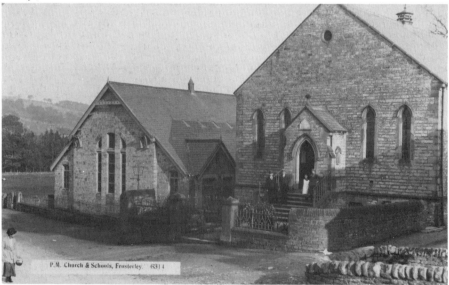

THE PRIMITIVE METHODIST SCHOOL, Bridge End, Frosterley, adjoins the chapel erected in 1861. It was intended mainly as a Sunday school and had partitions around its hall to enable separate classes to be held. It is now used by a local farmer. (Mrs M. Walton.)

AN EARLY GROUP of Weardale schoolmasters and schoolmistresses, c. 1895. It is thought this group was taken at a presentation. (Miss B. Backhouse.)

CLASS NO. 1, possibly at Eastgate School – a Weardale school group typical of many such photographs which survive in the Dale. What a pity that date, place and names are so often left unrecorded. (Mrs N. Brooksbank.)

LANEHEAD SCHOOL, 1934; an illustration of a vanishing species, a small village school serving the local community. (Mrs A. Dargue.)

SOME OF THE 46 PUPILS IN DALE HOUSE, one of the two houses into which the 86 pupils of Wolsingham Grammar School were divided in 1913 when Ella Parker (Mrs E. Wearmouth) was a pupil. There were 13 scholarship pupils; the rest were fee-paying. Mr Simms was the House Master and Miss Cheetham the House Mistress. Mrs Wearmouth can still remember many in her photograph: Maggie Weardale (Frosterley), C. Devey (Wolsingham), Edith Muschamp, Laurie Tinkler (Stanhope), Louisa Ellwood (Bollihope), Marie Leah Robson (Frosterley), Alfie Coulthard (Stanhope). The two boys at the front are the sons of Mr Joseph Backhouse, the Headmaster; they were not pupils but were privately educated. (Mrs E. Wearmouth.)

A CHEMISTRY PRACTICAL IN PROGRESS in the laboratory at Wolsingham Grammar School, c. 1946. While school groups are plentiful it is fairly uncommon to find an interior such as this, taken by Mr W.H. Lambert. (Durham County Reference Library.)

THE STAFF OF THE STANHOPE CASTLE SCHOOL, 1947, as drawn by Mr A. McKenzie and presented to colleague, Mr Merrick Jones. Opened in 1941, the approved school was a costly investment which caused Tom Sexton MP to table a question in the Commons. The total cost was £40,756; £6,123 the cost of the castle, £4,000 for equipment. The remaining £30,653 was for 'alterations and additions'. The cost of food, clothing and education was £18, £12 and £17 p.a. for each boy. (Miss M. Carrick.)

THE INTERNATIONAL INDEPENDENT DRUIDS was one of many such societies in the country designed to protect their members in times of sickness and unemployment. They usually commissioned a fine banner to be carried on special occasions. Photograph c. 1920, on Frosterley Green. (Mrs J. Gowland.)

BOLTSBURN FRIENDLY SOCIETY was a society with similar aims. This photograph shows its officers when it was re-formed in 1906. Before unemployment, sick pay, or the OAP, a working man's dread was that he might end up in the workhouse. Dr W. Robinson suggested that friendly societies should combine to establish a convalescent home for their members. This was done and a house opened at Grange-over-Sands. (Mr A. Blackburn.)

STANHOPE WORKHOUSE built in 1858 to the designs of W. Thompson contained a 'vagrants' wing where tramps could get a bed – at some cost! A pile of limestone would be tipped through the open iron doors into the sleeping cell; the vagrant would then have to break up the stones small enough for them to pass through the iron grid to the outside. Only then could he pull the bed down from the wall, be given a straw palliasse, and be allowed a meal. (Mr and Mrs Fellows.)

A WESLEYAN FRIENDLY SOCIETY, Stanhope, C. 1920, with its banner. J. Lonsdale, Jos Craig, Fenwick Coulthard, Arthur Henderson, A. Crooks, Jack Bainbridge, Jo lley of Bond Isle Farm and F. Coulthard junior are in the group. (Mrs E. Wearmouth.)

INITIATED BY PETER LEE, the Burnhope Reservoir scheme was approved in 1922 but shelved because of the Depression. In 1929 it was revived in response to the Government's appeal, backed by the promise of grant-aid, to create new jobs to relieve the grave unemployment problem. The reservoir provided employment for an average of 600 men during the five years of construction. A mini-village was erected and a temporary service railway was laid from Wearhead. Work on the reservoir began in July 1930 and it was formally opened on 15 September 1937 by Eli Cook JP. Mature and peaceful today, the reservoir is a haunt for walkers and fishermen. (Mrs E.E. Carrick.)

THE ENTERPRISE OF DR WILLIAM ROBINSON led to the founding of the Society for the Prevention and Cure of Consumption in 1898. A lease was taken on Horn Hall, Stanhope, which was fitted out as a sanatorium which opened in 1900 and was extended 1901–04. There was an emphasis on fresh air (hence the verandah and open-air shelters) and upon cleanliness and sound diet. Robinson was a remarkable man; a busy GP in an isolated area, he studied for his surgeon's qualification, researched on lead miners' diseases and kept up to date with the rapid advances in medicine. In 1894 he moved to Sunderland where he did equally enterprising work and research at the Eye Infirmary, and wrote its centenary history in 1936. At Stanhope he was succeeded by Dr John Gray of Ury House (now Glenroy). Dr Robinson died in 1940 when staying at Newtown Hotel, Stanhope; that year was the first time in 40 years that he had missed a meeting of the governors of the Sanatorium Society. He is buried in Stanhope churchyard. (W.M. Egglestone, 1916.)

The Hall, Holywood, Wolsingham. 5884

THE MATRON, Mrs Risbridger, and Medical Superintendent, Dr George Dodgson, stand on the terrace of Holywood Hall built by the industrialist Charles Attwood on his 400-acre estate. Purchased in 1905 by Durham County Council for £8,000, it was made into a 100-bed sanatorium. (Mrs J.H. Crosby.)

FRESH AIR was rightly regarded as a key factor in the treatment of TB, and open sleeping verandahs and cabins were installed at Holywood, Leazes, Wolsingham and Stanhope. These verandahs at Holywood were installed in 1916. (Mr and Mrs W.H. Holden.)

ST THOMAS OF CANTERBURY at Wolsingham is the only Roman Catholic Church to be built in the Dale since the Reformation. Designed by Joseph Hanson, it was dedicated on 5 September 1854, when relics of the patron saint were displayed upon the altar. The first priest was Father Thomas Wilkinson of Harperley Hall. There were then around 250 Catholics in the Dale; their numbers increased when many Catholics were among those incomers who sought employment at the steelworks. (Durham County Reference Library.)

MUCH WAS DONE BY FATHER WILKINSON to aid the Catholic Community. In 1892, the Sisters of Mercy from Sunderland founded a branch convent and school near the church. The school was for boarding and day girls; this is their schoolroom, c. 1914. (Mr and Mrs W.H. Holden.)

THE FINE CHURCH OF ST MARY AND ST STEPHEN, Wolsingham, c. 1942. The church was virtually rebuilt in 1848–9 to the design of a local man, William Nicholson. When re-opened, the church was dedicated anew to St Matthew but the original dedication was restored in 1896. The first known priest of Wolsingham was a William; he held 40 acres from the bishop in 1183. Since that time, the Church has played a prominent part in local affairs.

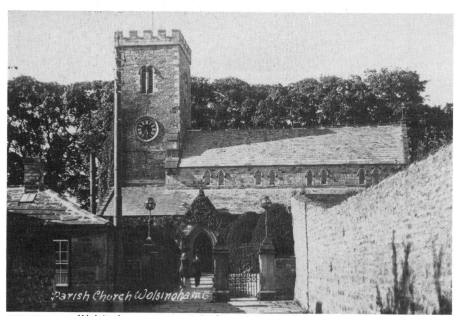

RECTORY LANE, Wolsingham, runs straight from the main street to the church in its lovely garth. The old Grammar School is at the top left; it is now a masonic hall. (Both Durham County Reference Library.)

A PHOTOGRAPH OF A DRAWING OF THE CHURCH at Wolsingham before the great rebuilding. Of this old building, the lower part of the tower and an internal door remain. Not everyone was pleased with the changes of 1848–9. Some lost their family pews as the galleries were not replaced. Also, graves were displaced. Forty years later, Amos Mitchell could still vividly recall rotting coffins being moved to a communal grave. (Durham County Reference Library.)

A GROUP CLUSTERED AROUND THE MARKET CROSS AT STANHOPE pose for their photograph around 1905; the new telegraph pole towers above them. Behind is the church of St Thomas the Apostle which has overlooked the Market Place for 790 years. Although heavily restored, 1866–8, it is clearly still a medieval building. (Mrs E. Hall.)

WILLIAM VINCENT RYAN, first Anglican Bishop of Mauritius, and John James Pulleine, Bishop of Richmond, are the only two of St Thomas' long line of distinguished rectors to be buried at Stanhope. For much of his Stanhope ministry (1883–88) Ryan was confined to a bath chair but nevertheless was an active pastor. Just before his death he insisted on visiting a fellow sufferer, Thomas Kemp, rectory gardener for 55 years. Photograph c. 1886. (Miss B. Backhouse.)

REVD PULLEINE, Rector 1888–1913 and Bishop from 1889, initiated several parish activities including a young men's organization such as the Methodists had. Here he is outside Stanhope Church, c. 1910, with a group which included Mr William Henry Bainbridge, father of Mr William Bainbridge, a headmaster of the Barrington School at Stanhope. (Mrs I. Bainbridge.)

THE INTERIOR OF ST THOMAS' CHURCH, Cowshill, when Canon Smith was vicar. Built in 1914 it replaced the old one of 1823 which was damaged beyond repair by quarrying on Copt Hill. A plaque commemorating Robert Maughan, vicar 1865–76, was given to the new church by Dr W. Robinson who composed the inscription: 'Tall and erect, he stood with noble mien, A scholar, gentleman and Christian'. Only half appeared on the plaque – the first part was judged 'unsuitable' for a church. Photograph 1953. (Mrs A. Dargue.)

'MY LOVELY HOME' is written on the back of this view of Cowshill with Copt Hill rising behind, c. 1935. It belonged to local postmaster Mr J.P. Carr. Mr Carr's son-in-law, Frank Mitchell, inscribed the fine scroll of the First World War dead in the church. Revd George Monkhouse was the first vicar to live in the new vicarage, seen left behind the church; his son Octavius kept the Cowshill Hotel and owned the Copt Hill whinstone quarry. (Mrs B. Monkhouse.)

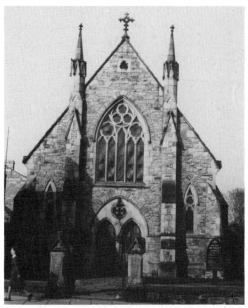

THE DEVELOPMENT OF METHODISM in Wolsingham followed the usual pattern: first the 'spark' was lit – here it was Wesley himself; house meetings followed. Then an early chapel; at Wolsingham it was in Whitfield Lane, which became known as Meeting House Lane. In 1836 a new chapel was built and later a school. In 1862 this chapel, the gift of Cuthbert Bainbridge and John Kirsop, was built next-door on the site of the Sun Inn. (Durham County Reference Library.)

CHRISTIAN ENDEAVOUR GROUPS figured prominently in 'chapel' activities before the Second World War. This Christian Endeavour Group is posing at Bridge End Farm, Frosterley in 1926. The stone farm with its Yorkshire sash windows was then farmed by Matthew Reed. The farmhouse has since been replaced by a new one. (Mrs L. Aberdeen.)

THIS HORSE-DRAWN MISSION CAR was dedicated to Joshua Dawson soon after his death in 1892. For a while it stood outside the door of his shop in the Market Place, St John's Chapel, as a token of respect. Joshua, an indefatigable missionary, preached only two days before his death, describing the occasion as 'the crowning day of my life'. His family presented an organ to High House Chapel in his memory; it was lovingly restored by Professor T.R. Milburn in 1984. (Weardale Museum.)

HARVEST HOME AT ROOKHOPE. Ever a popular festival of the Christian year, this photograph shows the great care and pride taken in decorating the chapel suitably for the occasion. (Mr A. Blackburn.)

VESTRY STONE LAYING at Lanehead Primitive Methodist Church, c. 1880. Though now reunited, the 'PMs' were a breakaway group of the Methodist Church. Most villages in the Dale have a building indicating their presence. Zion Chapel, Lanehead, built in 1834 and rebuilt in 1858, is one of the larger ones. The extension at the east end of the old chapel was given by his family as a memorial to Jonathan Humble and his son Oliver. The Lanehead Primitive and Wesleyan Methodists joined together in 1948; the Zion Chapel was closed.

Bottom right:
CHARLES HUMBLE'S PUBLIC HOUSE in Meadhope Street, Wolsingham, seen from the old pound or pinfold where straying animals were penned. Although sash windows have been inserted in the Black Lion, the stone mullion hoods of earlier (possibly seventeenth-century) windows remain on the upper storey. (Durham County Reference Library.)

STANHOPE WESLEYAN METHODIST SUNDAY SCHOOL, 1903–4. This photograph clearly demonstrates the strength of Methodism in the early years of this century. It also demonstrates the
memory of Mrs Ella Wearmouth of Stanhope, who celebrated her ninetieth birthday in the
Sunday School building behind the group, for she can remember many of the names
including, on the left, peeping between two boys wearing caps, Jo Wearmouth, her future
husband. Under the big hat is Lily Lonsdale, and Reuben Place is in the front row wearing a
sailor suit; Jack Bainbridge wearing a straw hat; Phoebe Bainbridge; Joseph Lonsdale with
Elsie in his arms. Mrs Wearmouth herself, then Ella Parker, is behind the 'bloomers', partially
hidden by the hat. (Mrs E. Wearmouth.)

THE BEAGLES AT THE PACK HORSE INN, STANHOPE. As well as Church and Chapel, the public house also offered diversions and the Dale had many of them. The Pack Horse was so named after the strings of Dales ponies which once carried loads of lead and iron ore down the Dale and this Market Place inn was a popular rest-stop. The Mews were its landlords for at least 30 years and the Mews Coach was kept there. Alfred Johnson was the landlord when this photograph was taken, c. 1930. (Mrs P. Craggs.)

THE ROOKHOPE INN, formerly the Commercial Inn, has served Rookhope and Boltsburn for at least 140 years. Pubs were not only drinking places but served as social clubs as well; darts, football and cricket teams often used them for meetings, especially before the institutes were built. (Mr K. Fairless.)

THE NATURAL SPORTS OF WEARDALE were chasing the deer, fox and hare, and shooting (or snaring) the pheasant and grouse (the 'bonny moor hen'). Beaters for the guns were always needed for the larger shooting parties and these beaters are helping with a shoot on Stanhope Moors in the late 1920s. (Mrs I. Bainbridge.)

THE HUNTSMAN with his beagles and hunt followers at a meet outside the Bay Horse Hotel, Upper Town, Wolsingham. Beagling still continues, though not so actively as 60 or 70 years ago, and the hare is not as common. (Durham County Reference Library.)

A WONDERFUL PHOTOGRAPH of the Stanhope Angling Club, c. 1905, owned by Mr J. Parmley whose great-grandfather Joseph Wallace (with beard) is among the group, which also includes Willie Tweddle. A trout licence cost 2s. (10p) at this time; a salmon one 5s. (25p). The Angling Club still functions and fishing is improving in the Dale as pollution declines. Unfortunately, there is sometimes trouble from unscrupulous 'professional' poachers. Modern anglers mostly use rods of fibre-glass or carbon fibre. The fishermen here would use greenheart or, possibly, split cane.

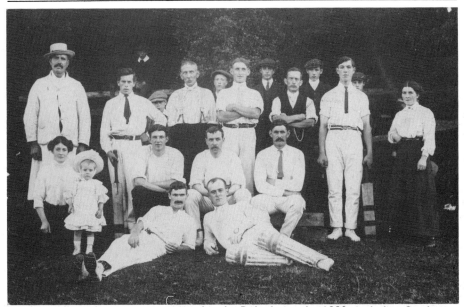

A NUMBER OF CRICKET CLUBS were started in the Dale during the 1880s including Stanhope, St John's Chapel, Rookhope, Frosterley and Wolsingham. This is Frosterley Cricket Club, date uncertain. At first, dress was informal but, by the mid-1930s, 'whites' were the rule. (Mrs M. Walton.)

A PRE-1914 PHOTOGRAPH of the first XI of Stanhope Men's Hockey Club. (Mr J. Parmley.)

Summer House, Stanhope Dene

A WALK IN STANHOPE DENE HAS ALWAYS BEEN POPULAR. Here, a man with his dog relaxes near the thatched summerhouse erected in the Dene as part of the improvements of 1891–2. The summerhouse and the bandstand were demolished before the war. (Mrs L. Aberdeen.)

A 'BEST DECORATED BICYCLE' COMPETITION was a favourite at inter-war garden parties and carnivals. This example comes from Frosterley, mid-1930s, when cloche hats and button strap shoes were popular. (Mrs M. Walton.)

NEW YEAR'S EVE was 'mischief day' for young people in the Dale; the mischief varied from village to village. At Rookhope (as shown here, around 70 years ago) every cart, barrow and trap they could find was dragged in front of the inn and 'ransomed' next day to their owners. (Mr A. Blackburn.)

A SCENE from the Frosterley Amateur Operatic Society's production of *Philide* or *Love on the Prairie*, c. 1934. A musical tradition is still strong in the Dale and the standard generally very high. (Mrs M. Walton.)

THREE DIGNIFIED BEEKEEPERS pose in front of their hives with smokers at the ready. It is thought that this photograph was taken at Low Bollihope and that the centre man is a Mr Greenwell, a local beekeeper around 1910. In spite of the delights of heather honey, bee keeping is not as widespread in the Dale as one might expect, although it is first mentioned in 1183 when Ralf held '6 acres for his service in keeping the bees'. (Mrs J.H. Crosby.)

THE STANHOPE SCOUT TROOP, c. 1935. Lord Baden-Powell initiated the scouting movement in 1907; the Stanhope group was founded c. 1922. Both Stanhope Scout and Cub troops were disbanded for the duration of the Second World War and were resumed in 1960 by the Rector, Canon Rodolphus Heselton. (Mr and Mrs S. Harrison.)

THE BOYS' BRIGADE outside Stanhope Castle, c. 1935. The Boys' Brigade was founded by William Alexander Smith in Glasgow in 1888 and did excellent work in many parts of the country. Willie Atkinson holds his walking stick; the Methodist minister is two places to his left. Sydney Wilkinson stands centre back and Albert Slack on the extreme right. Mr Tom Proud (centre front) was Brigade leader. (Mr and Mrs S. Harrison.)

FROSTERLEY WOMEN'S INSTITUTE FLOAT on carnival day. Mrs Mabel Robinson (extreme right back) and her fellow members dressed up as washerwomen and joined in the fun. (Mrs L. Aberdeen.)

THE 2ND VOLUNTEER BATTALION OF THE DURHAM LIGHT INFANTRY pose with their early Martini-Henry rifles in front of the Wheatsheaf, Cross Keys Inn and a thatched cottage in Wolsingham Market Place. The Cross Keys was taken over by the Mechanics Institute in 1888, so this photograph must be earlier than that. Some of the younger men in the group would have seen active service in the second Boer War of 1899–1902. (Mr G.S. Hindmarch.)

BELL AND BROWNBRIDGE'S BAKED-POTATO BARROW outside St Thomas' Church, Stanhope, at Christmas time, c. 1916. (Mrs E. Hall.)

WOLSINGHAM SILVER BAND, 1916 – part of a splendid brass band tradition begun in the Dale in 1824 with the formation of Stanhope Band by Joseph Fettes. The Wolsingham Band probably began in the late 1860s and practised in the Steelworks. The band's best year was 1916 and the conductor, Jimmy Elliott, was remembered as the man responsible, just as Jack Woodhall's name is still remembered in Stanhope as the man who led Stanhope Band to victory in the 1934 Crystal Palace competition. Wolsingham Band finished in 1948. Of the other Dale bands (Frosterley, Upper Weardale and two at Rookhope) only Stanhope, under Mr Stan Kell, remains to keep the brass tradition alive with the 'Plus Brass' ensemble adding to it since 1987. (Durham County Reference Library.)

A CHARMING PHOTOGRAPH of Mr J. Bell's mixed choir (and hats) taken in the Rectory garden, Wolsingham, c. 1912. Mr Bell was organist and choirmaster of St Thomas', Stanhope, and was also prominent in concerts and other musical events up and down the Dale. There is a plaque to his memory near the organ which he played in St Thomas'. (Mr J. Lumsden.)

THE ANNUAL AGRICULTURAL SHOWS AND CARNIVALS are the most important of the local high days and holidays. Wolsingham Agricultural Show, the oldest in the Dale, began around 1763. It was held in the Queen's Head with the livestock outside in the street. From 1862 it was held on the low-lying fields beside the river at West End, and moved to its present site in 1938. This photograph, taken from across the river c. 1905, shows the West End site, now partially occupied by the Recreation Ground. (Durham County Reference Library.)

Bottom, left:
MAKING MUSIC AT HOME, c. 1935. The Revd George Sharrock entertaining friends. Mr George Egglestone, son of William Morley Egglestone stands at back left; in front of him is Mr W.R. Currah. Such impromptu musical evenings around piano or harmonium were still a common occurrence before the Second World War and are not unknown now. (Mrs M. Wilkinson.)

JUDGING SHEEP at Stanhope Agricultural Show, 1930s. The Show began in the Market Place in 1834, moved to Fairfield in High Street and then to Castle Park. In 1947, anxious for his pupils' welfare, the Headmaster of Castle School stipulated no 'trot and scamper' racing and no betting, or no show. Racing and betting were cancelled but nevertheless record gate receipts of £1,250 were taken. In 1949 Unthank fields were purchased from the Hildyards and there the Show (with racing and betting) has continued ever since. (Mrs M. Wilkinson.)

THE AUTUMN MART AT WOLSINGHAM. A forlorn gatepost outside Wilsons, the seed merchants, is all that now survives of the Mart, shown here, c. 1930, when Mr Harry Pickering was auctioneer. Pickering was a prominent Wolsingham name. Florence, Emerson (Redgate Head), Thomas (Westfield) and Henry (East Newlands) were all farmers; Robert kept a grocer's shop. Chapel Mart is the only one to survive in the Dale now. (Durham County Reference Library.)

THE TERRITORIAL ARMY VOLUNTEERS practising at Stanhope station around 1910. Many of them went to war in earnest in 1914 in the Durham Light Infantry but in peace the TAs gave many men a satisfying spare-time occupation and companionship. (Mr J. Parmley.)

AN OUTING FOR WOUNDED AND CONVALESCENT SOLDIERS in the Market Place, St John's Chapel, c. 1917. One of the organizers, Octavius Monkhouse (with moustache, by the car) is prominent in his 'straw-banger'. Local people made many such efforts to comfort and entertain the war wounded sent to the Dale for nursing. (Mrs J.H. Crosby.)

ERECTING THE WAR MEMORIAL in Wolsingham in 1920. Made of Portland stone, the pedestal carries a carved celtic cross 17½ft high. It cost £500 – a large sum then for a small country town. 'Eight stone pillars with plain bronze rail' were placed around the memorial when completed; these were later removed. (Durham County Reference Library.)

THE MOUNTING OF A CAPTURED GERMAN GUN against Stanhope Police Station after the First World War was not kindly received by local ex-service men. A group of them manhandled the gun down to Stone Bridge and hurled it into the river, where it gradually broke up. This photograph was taken soon after the event. The barrel was later salvaged for scrap. Some of the men involved were locked up. A crowd of supporters gathered outside the station and so indicated their displeasure that the police thought it politic to release them. (Mrs D. Parker.)

A GIANT TREE against the churchyard wall had to be felled before the Stanhope war memorial could be erected. No wood-cutter would take the job because of the threat of damage to the wall, gravestones, telegraph wires and market cross. Although over 70 Thomas Gray, a woodsman and gamekeeper of legendary strength and skill, felled the tree single-handed and without damage to the surroundings. The memorial to the 33 dead was unveiled in 1920. (Mrs M. Walton.)

AN EARLY AEROPLANE in Stanhope Park in 1911 caused great excitement. The plane had great difficulty in taking off within the confines of the Park and had to be assisted by two men pushing the wings. The plane was part of the Stanhope Agricultural Show's festivities. Mr William John Ridley and Mr Jimmy Ridley are watching on the extreme right. (Mrs M. Wilkinson.)

MARGARET CURRAH AND ENA McKAY watch pieces of the fossil tree being assembled in the southern wall of the churchyard at Stanhope in 1962, at the instigation of Mr Beeston of The Poplars. In 1987 a party of German students from Bochum took an impression of the tree to exhibit in the museum there. (Mrs M. Wilkinson.)

LOCAL INCIDENTS always seem to attract a crowd as if by magic and the big fire, which partially destroyed the Bay Horse Hotel in Upper Town, Wolsingham, was no exception. The Pavilion Theatre alongside the hotel was a live theatre; later there was a cinema but both have long vanished. Photograph 1916. (Durham County Reference Library.)

A WEARDALE WEDDING, 14 September 1912, taken at the rear of the Featherstone home, now Barclay's Bank, St John's Chapel. From left to right: Jim Pentland senior, Jack Philipson, Mrs Henry Featherstone, Jim Pentland junior and Mabel Featherstone (groom and bride), Revd Penman (Wesleyan minister), Fanny Bell, Henry Featherstone – the 'grand old man of Weardale' and Jenny Carr. By careful annotation without damage to the original, Prof. T.R. Milburn shows us how old photographs should be preserved and identified.

MRS E. DAVISON on the float driven by her future husband, Eric, in the Victory Parade of 1945. There were parades such as this up and down the country as the end of six years of war was celebrated. (Mrs E. Davison.)

JOSEPH RACE, Methodist Minister in China, 1873–1880. 'Most of all I want to be a missionary' confided teenager Joseph to his brother Jack. A miner who had left Newhouse School at 12, Joseph nevertheless realized his dream. Work in the mission field was demanding and, at times, frustrating: 'We all want to be *useful* – if only the devil, the Secretaries and the Chairman will allow us', he stormed in 1878. He died of typhoid two years later. (Weardale Museum.)

JOHN RICHARD BLADES OF STANHOPE (b. 1894) represents all Dalesmen who fought in the First World War. Mr Blades returned to quarry work after the war but had to retire as he was riddled with shrapnel. He was a founder member of the Stanhope British Legion. He died in 1965, having been one of the last survivors of the 6th DLI Battalion which went to France early in 1915. (Mr and Mrs S. Harrison.)

'WHAT A WOMAN THIS WAS!' is written on the reverse of this photograph of Emma Jane McAlonan (1861–1945). The daughter of Joseph and Emma Jane Askew, she was born at Crawley Hall and later lived in Wolsingham. She and her husband were officers of William Booth's Salvation Army; together they served in Liverpool, Sweden, Germany and France. (Mr W.G. McAlonan.)

THESE WEARDALE PEOPLE were waiting on Stanhope station in 1904 for a train to begin the first stage of a 5,000-mile journey to the Mid-west Canadian Prairies. Uncertain job prospects in the Dale led many to emigrate, taking advantage of the cheap land and assisted passages. Prominent in the centre of the group is the Joshua Hodgson family with seven children; the eldest is Mary Jane in the fur-collared coat, the youngest in her mother's arms. Mary was soon married. At the age of 15 she married, at 7.30 p.m., Herbie McRorie, and 50 Dalesfolk joined in to have a 'fine and lively time of it' at the very first wedding in Perdue, Sask. Mary's mother was not overjoyed with her daughter. 'I think that the Mary Janes in our family get weaker and fonder (i.e., sillier) instead of weaker and wiser.' (Mr and Mrs S. Harrison.)

'I'VE MADE UP MY MIND to sail away, sail away, To the colonies I mean to stray' – so began a jingle composed by Tom Stephenson of Ravensfield, Stanhope. He left a recording on his phonograph (the only one then in Stanhope) and went off to Canada in 1904. Here he is with his wife Mary and her brother Amos Egglestone holding the draught oxen outside their turf farmhouse in Perdue, Saskatchewan. In spite of their new homeland, Weardale ties remained strong. When Amos died, 30 years later, his pall bearers were all 'Stanhope men'. (Mrs L. Aberdeen.)

SEARGEANT EDWARD ROWELL AND HIS WIFE, c. 1917. Edward Rowell left the Dale before the First World War and went to Australia where he worked in the mines. When war came, he returned home and enlisted in the army. He resettled in Australia after the war ended. (Mrs N. Brooksbank.)

TROOPS OF A DLI BATTALION at Wolsingham station waiting for a train to take them on the first stage to active service at the front, c. 1915. At first, weapons for training were in short supply and some letters home from camp mention drilling with broomsticks instead of rifles. The first Weardale man to enlist in the First World War was Mr A. Murdoch. He died on 11 November 1933 during the two minutes silence then observed throughout the country on Armistice Day. (Durham County Reference Library.)

A HAPPY NOTE ON WHICH TO END. Children from Weardale schools enjoying the summer camp at Whitley Bay, c. 1935. At the back is Miss Ella Parker (Mrs Wearmouth), Stanhope born and bred, who spent her teaching career in the Dale. Next to her is, first, Lizzie Wearmouth, then Elsie Bainbridge; Peggy McCollum (now Mrs Craggs, Verger of St Thomas') is two places along. In front of Miss Parker is Freda Priestman, then Gladys Forster, Jean Cleasby and Audrey Proud. In the front row at the left another Jean has been identified and, five and six places further along. Renée Sisson and Margaret Thompson, now Mrs Tuck. (Mrs E. Wearmouth.)

ACKNOWLEDGEMENTS

The response from friends old and new in providing illustrations for this book about Weardale has been wonderfully generous. There has indeed been an embarrassment of riches and this would still have been the case if the book had been four times the size. Unfortunately, all the photographs so kindly offered could not be used. Even the names of those who contributed would make a list too lengthy to be printed and there is always a chance that someone might be inadvertently omitted. So it is hoped that a warm general acknowledgement and the recording of the names of the owners beneath their photographs will suffice.

However, particular acknowledgement must be made under four headings to those who made an extraordinary contribution. Firstly, to fellow Trustees of the Weardale Museum of High House Chapel, notably Miss Barbara Backhouse, Miss Nellie Dawson, Professor Robert Milburn and Mr David Heatherington. Secondly, to Mr S. Dean, the County Librarian and his officer, Mr Ian Nelson, who allowed me to 'raid' the County Reference Library's collection of Weardale photographs; (many of these are from the collection of the late Mr J.H. Lambert). Thirdly, particular thanks are due to Mr Alan Blackburn of Rookhope Nurseries who gave me access to his collection. Lastly, but by no means least, to Mrs Lily Aberdeen whose encouragement, initiative and 'chauffeuring' kept me going.